Microsoft®
Publisher
for Office 365

TABLE OF CONTENTS

HOW TO USE THIS MANUAL

This manual was designed to be used as a reference. This is not a step-by-step tutorial. Our feeling is that students did not pay to have someone stand in front of class and read them something that they could do on their own. Through our own classroom experience, we have discovered that students don't read detailed descriptions and that lengthy text is ignored. They prefer to explore and try things out.

In typical tutorials, students often get lost following rote procedures and get caught in error conditions from which they can't back out of. Besides, once students leave class, they just want something they can use to look up a subject quickly without having to read through an entire tutorial. Our design ensures that each course is stimulating and customized yet covers the outlined objectives.

Keys and commands that you need to press are displayed as icons such as ENTER or ↑.

Each topic starts on a new page, making things easy to find and follow. In addition, topics covering actual commands always begin with the USAGE section where we explain the purpose of the command.

Publisher has different methods for accessing its commands: Students can use the keyboard, the mouse or their finger (if they are working with a touch screen device). Since the program was written to be used interactively with a mouse or your finger, the emphasis will be placed on those commands.

The next page shows how a typical topic will be discussed and each part found in the book.

THE TOPIC TITLE WILL BE ON TOP

USAGE:

This part of the manual explains what the command is used for, how it works and other miscellaneous information.

This icon indicates tools or buttons to click on with your mouse.

This part lists the keystrokes and function keys the user may press as a shortcut way of performing the command.

Microsoft Publisher supports a whole host of touch-screen gestures, including the swiping, pinching and rotating motions familiar to smartphone and tablet users. Tapping an item opens it; pressing and holding an item pops up a menu to display more information about it (similar to [RIGHT] clicking). This icon indicates a touch-screen gesture.

NOTE:	This box will tell of things to watch out for. The symbol in the left column always indicates an important note to remember.

TIP:	This box will let you in on a little secret or shortcut. The icon to the left always indicates a "TIP".

Module One

- **Running Publisher**
- **The Publisher Screen**
- **Getting Help**

RUNNING MICROSOFT PUBLISHER

USAGE:

Microsoft Publisher can be accessed through the Start menu, the Windows desktop or the taskbar (located along the bottom of the desktop window).

If you have pinned a shortcut to your desktop, double-click or tap the **Publisher** icon to run the application.

If you have pinned it to your taskbar, click on the Publisher icon:

If the Publisher icon isn't located on the desktop, you'll need to display all of your apps (from within the Start menu) to run it.

  Open the Start menu.

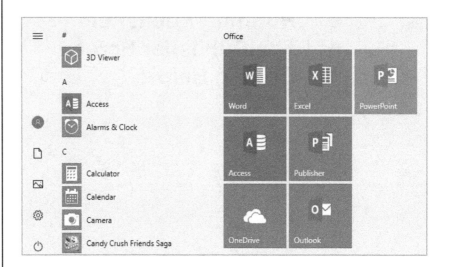

If it isn't already pinned to the Start menu (along the right), scroll through the alphabetical listing of installed apps or click on a letter to display an alphabetical index where you can quickly get to the app based on the first letter of its name.

THE OPENING SCREEN

When you first run the app, you'll be presented with the following screen:

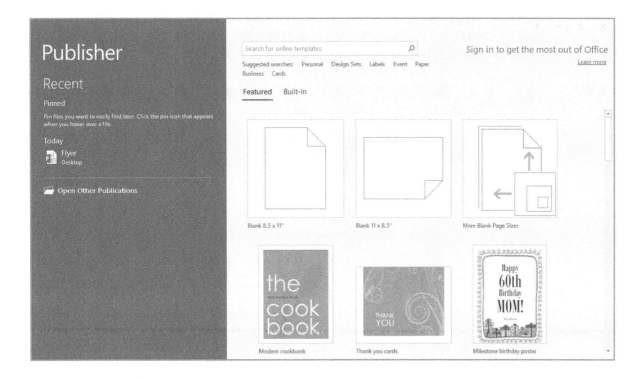

You can open a recently used publication, an older publication that has been stored on your system, or you can create a new publication based on of the many templates available.

If you don't see a template that matches the publication you want to create, you can search for one online.

If you want to create your own custom publication and not use any of Publisher's templates, simply select the "Blank" option that matches your paper size.

THE PUBLISHER SCREEN

You will notice that the program window includes many of the standard elements common to most Office 365 applications as well as a few items that are unique to Publisher. The screen can be quite intimidating the first time you see it as there are so many items displayed. However, if you take a few minutes to familiarize yourself with the various screen elements, the program will become easier to work with.

Along the top left corner of the screen is Save tool as well as the Undo and Redo tools. Since those are tools that are most often used, they are placed in a convenient location on what is referred to as the **Quick Access Toolbar**. Click or tap on the button to the right of these tools ⤓ to customize this Quick Access Toolbar.

The name of current publication followed by the application name is displayed in the middle. Until you save the file for the first time, Publisher assigns a generic file name for the new publication.

The far right side of title bar contains a section for signing in to your Microsoft account. There is also a Help button ?, along with three icons for minimizing, maximizing, and closing the program:

The second line (towards the left) contains tabs used to access a series of **Ribbons** to help you quickly find the commands needed to complete a task. Commands are organized in logical groups collected together under these tabs. Each tab relates to a type of activity. For example, the View tab contains tools to customize the view. To reduce clutter, some tabs are shown only when needed

To quickly collapse the Ribbon, press CTRL+F1. You can also click or tap on the ⌃ button (located to the far right side of the Ribbon). If you press CTRL+F1 a second time, the Ribbon will again be displayed. Even while collapsed, clicking or tapping on a tab will display the ribbon for that tab.

Touch screen users can click or tap on ⪦ (on the Quick Access Toolbar) and select Touch/Mouse Mode from the pull-down menu. A new tool will appear on the Quick Access toolbar. Click on 👆 ▾ and choose **Touch** from the pull-down menu to increase the space between buttons on the ribbon.

Use the ALT key to access the ribbon directly from the keyboard. For example, if you were to press ALT+N, you could access the "Insert" Ribbon. Each time you press ALT, Publisher displays corresponding letters for the ribbon items to help you to continue using keyboard shortcuts to select them.

Down the left side of the screen is the Page Navigation pane which allows you to move quickly through a multi-page publication.

The large interior portion of the window is referred to as the **Publication Window** and is where all of your work is performed. This is where you will enter the text and insert pictures and other objects that will make up your publication. Rulers are displayed across the top and down the left of the publication.

Publisher provides a page counter along the far left side of the **Status Bar** (located at the very bottom of the screen) which lets you know what page number you are currently viewing/working on

The bottom of the window contains the status bar which displays the current page number and viewing icons.

Page: 1 of 2   Clicking or tapping on this section toggles the page navigation pane on and off.

3.97, 5.87 in.   If nothing is currently selected, this section shows you the position of your mouse pointer. Once you
0.40, 0.39 in.   select an object, it displays the position of the selected object. If you click or tap in this section, Publisher will show the exact position of the selected object and allow you to change them.

2.82 x 5.10 in.   When an object is selected, this section displays its size. If you click or tap on this section, Publisher will show the exact measurements of the selected object and allow you to change them.

Click or tap on this icon (located towards the right side of the status bar) to view a single page at a time.

Click or tap on this icon (located towards the right side of the status bar) to view two pages at a time.

To the right of the view icons is the **Zoom** bar. Notice you can click or tap on the **+** button to increase or **–** button to decrease the viewing size of the publication. You can also drag the slider horizontally to change the text size as it appears on the screen. Publisher displays the current percentage to the right of this area.

Click or tap on this icon (located along the far right side of the status bar) to view a full page at once.

Microsoft Publisher for Office 365

WORKING WITH HELP

USAGE:

Publisher has an extensive help database that can assist you with virtually any topic you encounter while working with the program.

Help can be as generic as explaining how to print within the program or as specific as detailing each item within a dialog box.

? To display help, simply click or tap on this tool (located on the far right side of the tabs and just above the Ribbon).

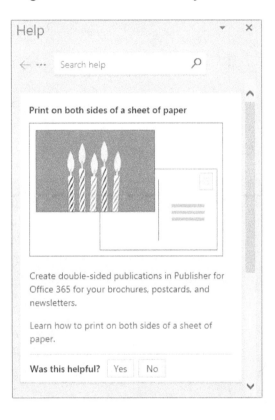

Click or tap in this box to enter a new search topic.

← Click on this arrow to return to the previous help screen.

… Click on the three dots (…) to display a pull-down menu with the following items:

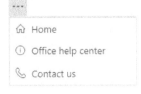

©2019 EZ-REF Courseware   **Page 7**

At the end of each help topic, you will see two items:

One item will allow you to send feedback to Microsoft as to whether the information contained within the help panel was helpful:

Was this helpful? Yes   No

After answering the question, you can also include a comment as part of the feedback you are sending Microsoft:

Great! Any other feedback?

To protect your privacy, please do not include contact information in your feedback. Review our privacy policy.

Send   No thanks

Some articles may also include this item (at the bottom of the help panel) which allows you to launch your Internet browser and view more detailed information on the currently selected topic through Microsoft's support website:

Read article in browser ↗

You can then use your browser's print option if you'd like to print out information on the selected topic.

EXITING HELP

✕ Click or tap on this button (located in the top right corner) to **close** the help window and return to your publication.

SCREENTIPS

A common problem most users encounter is not knowing what each tool on the screen represents.

For example, the SAVE tool is displayed as a 3.5" diskette which some users do not immediately relate to saving a file.

To alleviate this problem, Publisher offers quick mouse assistance on each tool, referred to as ScreenTips.

As you point to a tool, Publisher will display a quick note as to the tool's function.

Paste (Ctrl+V)

Add content on the Clipboard to your document.

PRACTICE EXERCISE

Instructions:	❶	Using help, find out what's new in Publisher.
	❷	If you are connected to a printer, print the help section containing the major new changes.
	❸	Find the help topic on how to add page borders. Again, if you are connected to a printer, print the information out for future reference.

Module Two

- **Creating a New Publication**
- **Viewing Options**
- **Saving & Spell Checking**
- **Changing Publication Options**
- **Inserting & Deleting Pages**
- **Adding Page Numbers**
- **Working with Headers & Footers**
- **Inserting a Section**
- **Working with Layout & Ruler Guides**
- **Changing the Page Setup**
- **Previewing & Printing**
- **Closing a Publication**

CREATING A NEW PUBLICATION

USAGE:

You can use Publisher to create brochures, newsletters, greeting cards, and a host of other items. By selecting one of the predefined templates, all you will need to do is enter the text since the layout and formatting will be done for you.

To create a new publication, follow these steps:

❶   From within the **File Ribbon**, select **New**.

The following screen will be displayed:

Notice that you can create a blank publication or base the new file on one of the built-in templates that come with Publisher. A template is used to determine the basic structure of the publication and can contain predefined settings, such as colors, fonts, layouts, graphics, formatting, and macros.

When you click or tap on one of the templates, a pop-up window is displayed with a preview of the template and a short description. If you don't see a template that you want to use, you can select a different category.

If there are templates that you'll be using on a regular basis, you may want to pin them to the list so that they remain at the top for easy access.

 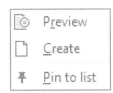

To quickly pin a template, point to the template and then click or tap on ⚲ (located along the bottom right corner of its preview) or click your [RIGHT] mouse button once and choose **Pin to list** from the pop-up menu.

If you change your mind, click or tap on the ⚲ icon (located on the template preview) to unpin the template.

❷ Select one of the categories (Brochure, Label, Card, Certificate, Flyer) or enter keywords in the box provided if you want to search for a completely different category. Publisher will open a second window (along the right side of your screen) listing all of the available categories from which to choose.

❸ Select the category and then click/tap the actual template (from within the selected category) to base the new publication on.

❹ When ready, click or tap on the [Create] button.

The new publication will be created - based on the template you have selected.

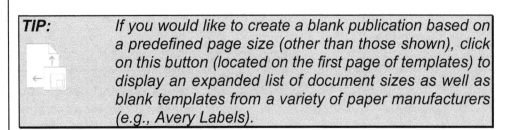

TIP: *If you would like to create a blank publication based on a predefined page size (other than those shown), click on this button (located on the first page of templates) to display an expanded list of document sizes as well as blank templates from a variety of paper manufacturers (e.g., Avery Labels).*

VIEWING OPTIONS

USAGE:

While working with a publication, you should know how to switch views and quickly navigate through it.

- **-**   Click or tap this tool (located on the status bar) to **zoom out** of the publication. Each time you click on this tool, Publisher will zoom out - making the page appear smaller and smaller.

- **+**   Click or tap this tool (located on the status bar) to **zoom in** to the publication. Each time you click on this tool, Publisher will zoom in - making the page appear larger and larger.

 Click or tap on this tool (located within the Zoom section on the **View Ribbon**) to switch to 100%.

 Click or tap on this tool (located within the Zoom section on the **View Ribbon**) to zoom the document so an entire page fits in a window.

 Click or tap on this tool (located within the Zoom section on the **View Ribbon**) to zoom the document so the width of the page fits the width of the window.

 Use this tool (located within the Zoom section on the **View Ribbon**) to select a specific zoom level.

SWITCHING BETWEEN MULTIPLE PUBLICATIONS

 When working with two or more open publications, you can access the **View Ribbon** and then switch between windows or you can quickly switch between open publications using the Windows taskbar along the bottom of your screen.

Each time you create a new publication or open an existing one, Publisher stacks them on top of one another along your taskbar - making it easy to access. Simply point to the stacked icon and select the publication you want to switch to from the pop-up list:

DISPLAYING NON-PRINTING SYMBOLS

¶ This tool (located within the Paragraph section on the **Home Ribbon**) toggles between displaying/hiding non-printing symbols, such as hard returns and spaces.

SINGLE PAGE AND TWO-PAGE SPREAD

If you are working with multiple pages, you might want to display two pages at once to see how they will print. This is especially useful when creating a multi-page brochure or booklet.

Two-Page Spread

To switch to two pages, click or tap on this tool (located within the Layout section of the **View** ribbon).

Single Page

To switch back to a single page view, click or tap on this tool (located within the Layout section of the **View** ribbon).

VIEWING/HIDING THE RULER

If you are working with text boxes or trying to align other objects on a page, you will probably want the rulers displayed across the top and along the left side of the screen.

☑ Rulers   If the rulers are not currently displayed, check this box (located within the Show section of the **View Ribbon**).

To remove the rulers from the screen, simply remove the check from the box.

VIEWING/HIDING THE BOUNDARIES AND GUIDES

By default, Publisher displays layout guides, ruler guides and object boundaries so that you can see exactly where each object is placed on the page.

☐ Boundaries

☐ Guides   If the boundaries and guides are not currently displayed, you can display them by checking these boxes (located within the Show section of the **View Ribbon**).

To remove the boundaries and guides from view, simply remove the checkmarks from the boxes.

SELECTING OBJECTS

USAGE:

Once objects have been added to a publication, you must select them before modification is possible.

Publisher allows you to move, copy, resize, delete and change the color of a selected object. If the object contains text, you can also edit the font and size of the text, as well as any attributes that may have been applied.

SELECTING AN INDIVIDUAL OBJECT

To select an object, follow these two steps:

 Move to the middle of the graphic object you want to select or the border of the text item. Once you see the pointer change to a four-way arrow, click the **[LEFT]** mouse button.

An object is selected when it has the outline of a box with small handles surrounding it.

SELECTING MULTIPLE OBJECTS

To select multiple objects, click on the first object and then hold the **SHIFT** key down while clicking on the additional objects.

> **NOTE:** *If you click on an object a second time (while holding* **SHIFT** *down), you will be deselecting that object.*

SELECTING ALL

To select all objects on a page or the entire story within the currently selected text box:

Press **CTRL** + **A**

If you were in the middle of editing a text box (story), the entire story would now be selected. If you were not editing a text box, all objects on the current page would be selected.

SAVING A PUBLICATION

USAGE:

After having created a publication, you will want to save it and assign a name so that you can easily find it again. There are two main options for saving a publication: **Save** and **Save As**.

SAVE is the normal save feature which will ask you the first time you save a file to assign a name to it. From that point on, choosing SAVE will simply update the file to include the new information. On the other hand, **SAVE AS** saves an existing file under a new name or as a different format to be imported into another program.

 Click or tap the **Save** tool (located on the Quick Access Bar).

When you first save a publication, you will need to specify where you want to save it:

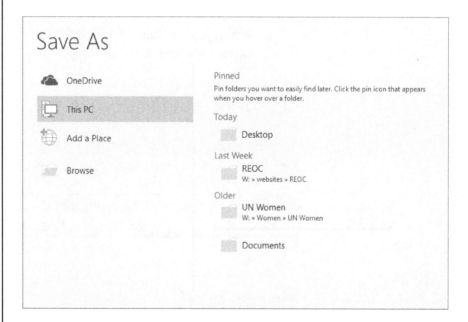

 OneDrive — Use this if you want to store the publication on the Internet rather than a local computer. This allows you to access the file from anywhere.

 This PC — Use this option to save the publication in a folder on your local computer – which may also include network locations.

 Add a Place — Use this to add a SharePoint location.

Browse

If you're storing the publication on your local computer, you can choose from the list of recently accessed folders or click on the Browse button to search your system for the location.

Once you select a storage location, you will be taken to the dialog box that will prompt you to enter a file name, as shown below:

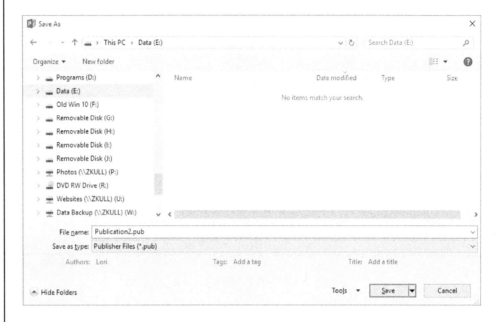

Along the left side of the dialog box, Publisher displays the **Navigation Pane**. This pane lists common/favorite locations (links) as well as a section for browsing your folders and drives.

You can hide/display the "Folders List" section at the bottom of this area by clicking or tapping on the ∨ ∧ arrows.

Use the address bar to determine the path, as shown below:

Notice the path is displayed horizontally on the bar. For example, in the diagram shown above the currently selected item is the "Data" drive (E:). To get to that folder, you had to first go to "This PC", then the Data drive (E).

This layout is commonly referred to as "bread crumbs" because it shows you the path that was taken to get to the current location.

You can easily move to another folder on the "E" drive by clicking or tapping on the ⟩ arrow beside the drive name and then selecting a different folder to view.

In the box labeled "**File name**", enter a name for the new file. Letters, numbers and spaces are allowed. Enter 1-255 characters.

Notice that Publisher defaults to assigning the "pub" extension. This is to identify it as a "Microsoft Publisher" file which has a specific format.

If you want to save the publication in another format (such as a previous version of Publisher so that someone else can edit the document who does not have this version), click or tap on the down arrow ⌄ beside the box labeled **Save as type** and select the format from the list provided.

When ready, click or tap [Save] to actually save the publication.

TIP:	The shortcut key for saving while working within the publication is [CTRL]+[S].

USING THE AUTO SPELL CHECKER

USAGE:

Publisher offers an automatic spell checker which, as you type, checks words to see if they match the installed dictionary. If you type a word that is not included in the installed dictionary, Publisher will flag it as a misspelling by underlining it in red. The underline is for viewing purposes only and will not be printed.

This is a sentence with a mstake in it.

You can quickly correct the spelling mistake using your mouse.

Click the **[RIGHT]** mouse button (or tap and hold if using a touch screen device) while pointing to the flagged word.

A pop-up menu will appear as shown below:

The top portion of the pop-up menu offers suggestions for the flagged word. Notice that Publisher also allows you to **ignore** the word (regardless of how many times it is contained within the document) or **add** the word to the user dictionary for future reference.

You can also instruct Publisher to change the proofing **language** that is being used to check the spelling. In addition, you can access the **spelling** dialog box or **lookup** the word.

USING THE SPELL CHECKER

USAGE:

Before printing and sending a publication out for others to read, you should always spell check it for typing errors. By comparing words in your file against the dictionary, Publisher can check your spelling and alert you of possible mistakes.

For each word the program cannot find in its dictionary, Publisher asks what you want to do. You will be able to choose to change the spelling, suggest alternative words, leave the word as it is, or add the word to the dictionary.

Publisher also checks for words that are incorrectly capitalized and for repeated words.

ABC
✓
Spelling

Click or tap on the **Spelling** tool (located within the Proofing section on the Review Ribbon).

Publisher will display the following box:

Check Spelling: English (United States)	? ✕
Not in dictionary:	
quotees	Ignore Ignore All
	Change Change All
Change to: quotes	Add Close
Suggestions: quotes	
	☐ Check all stories
	Options ...

The following buttons are provided within the spell-checking panel:

Ignore / Ignore All	If the word should remain as it is, select the **Ignore** button. Publisher also offers the option of **Ignore All** if the word in question appears throughout the publication.
Add	If the word should be added to your custom dictionary for future reference, click or tap on this button.
Change / Change All	If one of the suggestions is correct, double-click or double-tap on the correct spelling or highlight the word and choose the **Change** button. If you are afraid you misspelled a word more than once, click or tap on the **Change All** button.
☐ Check all stories	Check this box to have Publisher check the entire publication rather than just the current text box.

Options... This button is used to change the options associated with spelling features.

> **ABC✓** Change how Publisher corrects and formats text.
>
> **AutoCorrect options**
>
> Change how Publisher corrects and formats text as you type: **AutoCorrect Options...**
>
> **When correcting spelling in Microsoft Office programs**
>
> ☑ Ignore words in UPPERCASE
> ☑ Ignore words that contain numbers
> ☑ Ignore Internet and file addresses
> ☑ Flag repeated words
> ☐ Enforce accented uppercase in French
> ☐ Suggest from main dictionary only
>
> Custom Dictionaries...
>
> French modes: Traditional and new spellings ▾
> Spanish modes: Tuteo verb forms only ▾
>
> **When correcting spelling in Publisher**
>
> ☑ Check spelling as you type
> ☐ Hide spelling and grammar errors

This box provides a variety of options to customize how the spell checker works. You can specify whether to suggest and where to get the suggestions and what you want to ignore during the spell checker (such as uppercase words or words containing numbers).

Click or tap on **Custom Dictionaries...** to add or modify custom dictionaries, such as medical and legal to be used during spell checking.

Once all options are selected, choose **OK**. You will be returned to the original spell-checking box where you can continue.

After running the spell checker, save your publication again.

CHANGING PUBLICATION OPTIONS

USAGE:

Regardless of what type of publication you are currently working on, you can change the color scheme, the font scheme and the publication template that is being applied to the document.

APPLYING A NEW DESIGN TEMPLATE

While working with a publication, you may decide that a different design template would have looked better.

Rather than starting over from scratch, you can quickly apply a different design to the current publication. However, if the new template is substantially different than your existing one, you may find that you will need to do a lot of work to re-create your publication.

To apply a new design template to the publication you are currently working on, follow these steps:

❶ Change Template
Click or tap on this tool (located within the **Template** section on the Page Design Ribbon).

❷ The "Change template" window will open:

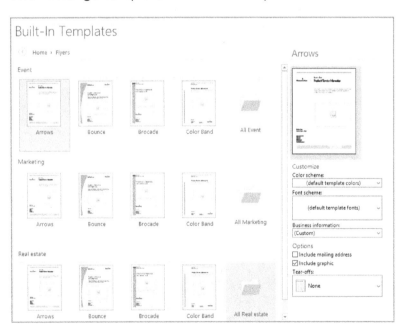

Select the new template and click or tap OK .

❸   You will be asked whether you want to change the current publication or create a new one based on the selected template. Choose **Apply template to the current publication** and click or tap [OK].

Your publication will change to display the options for the newly selected template.

> **NOTE:**   *If the new template cannot fit all of the objects of your publication, the "Extra Content" pane will be opened along the right side of your screen. Using this pane, you can reinsert the objects.*

APPLYING A NEW COLOR SCHEME

Publisher automatically selects a color scheme for each publication you create based on the one stored with the selected template.

If for some reason, you want to apply a different color scheme to the current publication, select the new set of colors from the **Schemes** section on the Page Design Ribbon:

Apex	Aspect	Black & ...	Civic
Concourse	Equity	Flow	Foundry
Median	Metro	Module	Office

> **NOTE:**   *If you want to create your own custom color scheme, click or tap on the down arrow ⊡ beside the list of schemes and select the **Create New Color Scheme...** option at the bottom of the list. You will be taken to a dialog box where you can create your own custom color schemes.*

APPLYING A NEW FONT SCHEME

Publisher automatically selects a font scheme for each publication you create based on the type of publication and design template you have selected.

If for some reason, you want to apply a different font scheme to the current publication, follow these steps:

❶ Click or tap on this tool (located within the **Schemes** section of the Page Design Ribbon).

Fonts

❷  From the list, choose the scheme you would like applied to your publication.

NOTE: *Notice you can also create your own font scheme.*

*If you want to update any custom font styles you may have created, override text formatting you may have applied and/or adjust the font sizes within your publication based on the new scheme, click on **Font Scheme Options...** You'll be taken to a dialog box where you can make the updates.*

APPLYING A BACKGROUND

In addition to applying a design template to your publication, you can also assign a background color, pattern, gradient, picture, texture, or tint. These background elements can help to customize your publication.

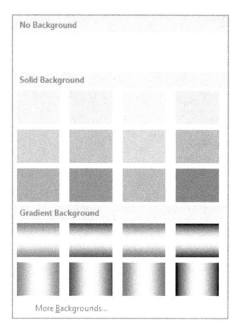

Click or tap on this tool (located within the **Page Background** section of the Page Design Ribbon).

From the list, select the background you wish to apply to your publication.

The color options within this pull-down list will vary, depending on what template and color scheme you are using.

INSERTING A PAGE

USAGE:

When creating a publication, you may decide you need more than a single page.

Page

Click or tap on this tool (located within the **Pages** section of the Insert Ribbon).

```
📄  Insert Blank Page
    Insert Duplicate Page
    Insert Page...
```

From the pull-down menu, select whether you want to insert a blank page or a duplicate page.

If you select the last item within the pull-down list (**Insert Page...**), the following dialog box will be displayed:

You'll be asked the number of new pages to insert, where the new pages should be placed within the publication (before or after the current page), and the type of page to insert (no objects on the new pages, one text box per page or all objects duplicated from an existing page). The **Master page** option will be displayed if you are using a template.

When done with all settings, click or tap on [OK] to actually insert the new page(s).

DELETING A PAGE

USAGE:

If have multiple pages and decide that one of the pages needs to be removed from your publication, you can easily delete it.

To delete a page, move to the page you want to remove.

[x] Delete   Click or tap on this tool (located within the **Pages** section on the Page Design Ribbon).

If the page you are deleting contains data, you will be warned that deleting the page will result in also deleting all objects contained on the page:

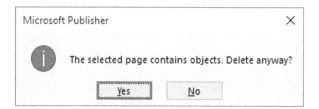

After reading the confirmation warning, click or tap [Yes] to actually delete the current page and all of its contents.

If the page does not contain data, Publisher will remove it from your publication without first warning you of data loss.

INSERTING PAGE NUMBERS

USAGE:

If you are creating a booklet with multiple pages, you will probably want the pages to be numbered.

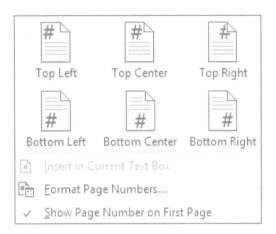

Click or tap on this tool (located within the **Header & Footer** section on the Insert Ribbon) to insert page numbers within your publication.

From the pull-down list, select the position on the page where the numbers should be placed.

Notice you can also insert the number within a text box and also format the numbers.

The final option allows you to specify whether the first page of the publication should include a page number.

WORKING WITH HEADERS AND FOOTERS

USAGE:

Headers are placed at the top of every page and can be used for adding chapter/book titles or any other text that should be printed at the head (top) of every page.

Footers, on the other hand, are placed at the bottom of every page and are most commonly used for adding custom page numbers or any other text that should be placed at the foot (bottom) of every page within a publication.

Headers are printed within the top margin of the publication while footers are printed within the bottom margin.

INSERTING HEADERS AND FOOTERS

To insert a header or footer, click or tap on one of these tools (located within the **Header & Footer** section of the Insert Ribbon).

If you chose to insert a header, the screen will change to display a text box labeled **Header**, as illustrated below:

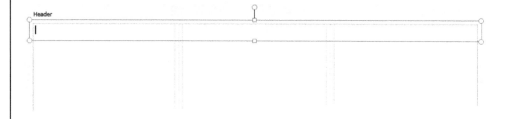

Simply enter the text you would like to be printed at the top (head) of each page within your publication.

Notice the rotation handle at the top of the header box - which allows you to rotate the header box just as you would any other text box within Publisher.

When working with headers and footers, the Master Page Ribbon will be displayed containing a set of Header & Footer tools:

Show Header/ Insert Page Insert Insert
Footer   Number   Date   Time

Show Header/
Footer

Use this tool to switch between the header and footer.

Insert Page
Number

This tool inserts the current page number.

Insert
Date

Click or tap on this tool to insert the current date in the header or footer.

Insert
Time

This tool inserts the current time in the header or footer.

Close
Master Page

When done, click or tap this tool to remove the toolbar from the screen and close the header or footer window.

EDITING THE HEADER OR FOOTER

To edit an existing header or footer, simply double-click or double-tap on the header/footer text. You will be returned to the header/footer window where you may immediately begin editing the existing text and/or graphics that make up your header/footer.

DELETING A HEADER OR FOOTER

To remove an existing header or footer, simply choose to edit it and then delete the contents of the header/footer box.

WORKING WITH LAYOUT & RULER GUIDES

USAGE:

Layout guides are available within Publisher to create common margins and boundaries that repeat on each page so that you can easily align your text, pictures, and other objects into columns and rows to give your file a more uniform look.

Ruler guides can be then added to individual pages for special formatting requirements.

 Guides

Click or tap on this tool (located within the **Layout** section of the Page Design Ribbon)

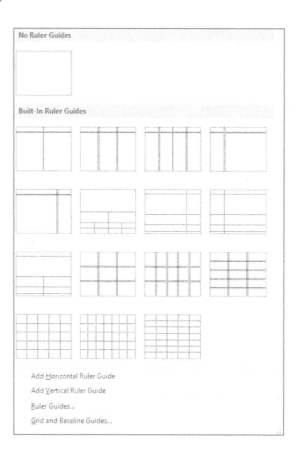

Select one of the built-in ruler guides from the pull-down list or manually add a horizontal or vertical ruler guide.

There are two options located at the bottom of the pull-down list:

Ruler Guides   Select this option to access a dialog box where you can specify the horizontal and vertical ruler guide position.

Grid and Baseline Guides   This option allows you to customize margin, grid and baseline guides. You'll be taken to a dialog box containing three tabs.

ADDING A RULER GUIDE

To add a vertical or horizontal ruler guide to a specific location on your page, follow these three steps:

❶   Point to the top or left ruler until your pointer changes to ⬍ or ⬌ . Notice that with the arrows, Publisher displays the message **Create Vertical Guide** or **Create Horizontal Guide** to let you know which you are about to create.

❷   Click within the ruler and then drag the mouse to the page location where the ruler guide should be placed. A thin line will represent the ruler guide you are creating.

❸   When done, release the mouse button.

REPOSITIONING A RULER GUIDE

If you decide you need to move a ruler guide to a new location on your page, point to the guide and begin dragging it to its new location.

When done, release the mouse button.

REMOVING A RULER GUIDE

If you decide that you no longer need a ruler guide, you can remove it from your page by dragging it back to the ruler.

REPOSITIONING THE RULER

You can reposition either the horizontal or vertical ruler to a new location on your page by pointing to the ruler and begin dragging it - while holding down the SHIFT key, to its new location.

When done, release the mouse button and the SHIFT key.

CHANGING YOUR PAGE SETUP

USAGE:

Before printing, you may want to take a few minutes to be sure that the page setup options (such as publication size, paper size, and orientation) have been properly defined.

To modify the page setup options, access the following menu:

CHANGING MARGINS

Margins

Click or tap on the **Margins** tool (located within the **Page Setup** section on the Page Design Ribbon).

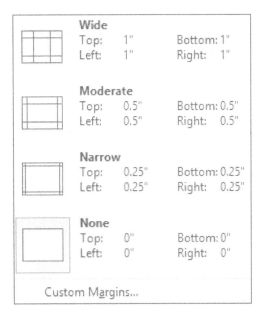

Select the new margin setting from the list provided.

If you need a margin setting that is not included in this pull-down list, click or tap on **Customize Margins….** (located at the bottom of the list) to open a dialog box where you can enter custom margins.

CHANGING ORIENTATION

Orientation

Click on the **Orientation** tool (located within the **Page Setup** section on the Page Design Ribbon).

📄 Portrait

📄 Landscape

Select the page orientation from the two diagrams provided.

CHANGING PAPER SIZE

Size

Click or tap on the **Size** tool (located within the **Page Setup** section on the Page Design Ribbon).

Built-In

A3 (Landscape)
16.535 x 11.693"

A4 (Landscape)
11.693 x 8.268"

A5 (Landscape)
8.268 x 5.827"

B4 (Landscape)
13.898 x 9.843"

B5 (Landscape)
9.843 x 6.929"

Executive (Landscape)
10.5 x 7.25"

Legal (Landscape)
14 x 8.5"

Letter (Landscape)
11 x 8.5"

Tabloid (Landscape)
17 x 11"

Page Setup...

Create New Page Size...

More Preset Page Sizes...

Select the paper size desired. If you don't see a size in the list, click or tap **More Preset Page Sizes…**

PRINTING YOUR PUBLICATION

USAGE:

You can choose what part of the publication you want to print (such as the current page, multiple pages or the entire file). In addition, you can specify which printer to use and how many copies to print.

Click or tap on the **File** tab on the Ribbon and select **Print** from the pull-down list of options.

The Print window will be displayed:

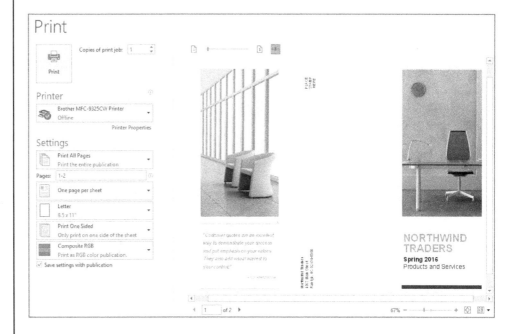

A preview of the publication as it will be printed appears along the right side of this window.

⌐ᵢ⌐ ┼────────────── ⌐ᵢ⌐	Use this slider (located across the top of the preview pane) to display page numbers (only as a reference to yourself while viewing a large publication). The slider is used to make the numbers lighter or darker but are not printed
⊦8⊦	Click or tap on this button (also located across the top of the preview pane) to toggle the page rulers on and off which will display the page dimensions.
◀ 5 of 15 ▶	Use this section (located along the bottom left of the preview pane) to display a specific page within your publication.
56% ─ ──┼──┼── +	Use this section (located along the bottom right of the preview window) to zoom in and out of the publication.
⟨□⟩	Use this button (located to the right of the zoom section along the bottom of the preview pane) to quickly display the full page.
🆗 ▼	Click or tap on this button to display multiple pages – which can be useful for reviewing the overall layout.
Copies of print job: 1 ▲▼	Use this section to specify how many copies you'd like to print.
Brother HL-2170W Ready	Click or tap on this button to select the printer you want to use.

Printer Properties

Click or tap this item to access additional properties for the printout.

Settings

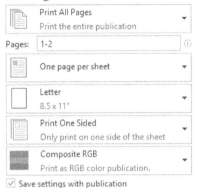

Use this section to specify print settings, such as which page(s) to print, what size paper you're printing on and whether you're printing on both sides of the sheet.

Print All Pages	Print the entire publication
Pages:	1-2
One page per sheet	
Letter	8.5 x 11"
Print One Sided	Only print on one side of the sheet
Composite RGB	Print as RGB color publication.

☑ Save settings with publication

Print

Once all settings have been made, click or tap on this button to begin printing.

TIP: *You can quickly access the print dialog box from within your publication by pressing [CTRL]+[P].*

CLOSING A PUBLICATION

USAGE:

Although you can have several windows (publications) open at the same time, it is usually a good idea to close a publication once you have saved and printed it if you no longer need to continue editing.

✕   Click or tap on the close button in the upper right corner of the window to close the current document. If you only have one publication open and you click on this icon, Publisher will close the entire program.

If you only have one publication open and don't want to close the entire application, you can close the publication by accessing the **File** tab on the Ribbon, as shown below:

Select **Close** from the pull-down list of options.

NOTE:	If you have made changes to the publication and have not saved those changes, Publisher will ask whether you want to save the changes before closing the file.

PRACTICE EXERCISE

Instructions:

❶ Create a flyer using any of the templates available within Publisher. Add your company name and a few lines of text describing the product or service that your company offers. Feel free to make up any information you want.

❷ Spell check the file to locate any mistakes you may have made.

❸ Save the file as **Product Flyer**

❹ Print (or preview) the publication.

❺ Close the publication.

PRACTICE EXERCISE

Instructions:

❶ Create a brochure using any of the templates available within Publisher. Add fictitious information describing an upcoming event. Feel free to make up any information you want.

❷ Spell check the file to locate any mistakes you may have made.

❸ Save the file as **My Brochure**.

❹ Change the design template assigned to the brochure.

❺ Select a new color scheme for your publication.

❻ Choose a new font scheme as well.

❼ Print (or preview) the publication.

❽ Close the publication.

Module Three

- **Opening a Publication**
- **Working with Text**
- **Applying Attributes & Changing Fonts**
- **Using the Ruler & Measurement Toolbar**
- **Formatting with DropCaps**
- **Finding & Replacing Text**
- **Working with the Thesaurus**
- **Editing Text Using MS Word**
- **Importing a Word Document**
- **Inserting the Date & Time**
- **Adding Symbols**
- **Moving & Copying Objects**
- **Working with the Office Clipboard**
- **Resizing & Deleting Objects**
- **Rotating Objects**
- **Working with Layers**

OPENING AN EXISTING PUBLICATION

USAGE:

Whenever you want to work on a publication that already exists, you will need to open it. There are several ways to open a file.

To open an existing publication, select **Open** from the pull-down list of options within the File tab on the Ribbon.

If you select the option labeled **Recent** from this list, you will be taken to a box displaying your most recently used files.

The following window will be displayed:

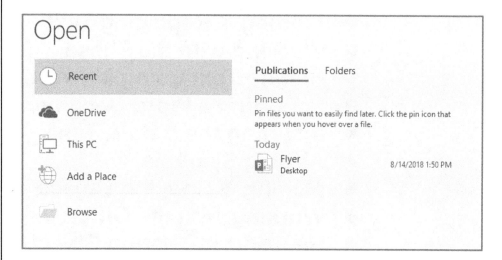

Notice your most recently accessed publication files are automatically listed in this window.

Your first step is to select the location where the file is stored:

 Recent
This is the default option. Publisher automatically displays files you have recently been working on so that you can quickly return to them.

 OneDrive
Use this if you want to open a publication that has been stored on the Internet rather than a local computer.

 This PC
Use this option to open a publication that was stored in a folder on your local computer – which may also include network locations.

 Add a Place
Use this to add a new SharePoint location from which to open files.

TIP: *If there are files or folders that you access often, you can "**pin**" them to the list so that they are always available, whenever you access the Open dialog box.*

To pin a file/folder, point to it (from within the list) and then click on the icon.

If you change your mind and no longer need the file/folder pinned to the list, point to the item and then click or tap on ⊤ to remove it.

Browse
If you're opening a publication that was stored on your local computer, you can choose from the list of recently accessed folders or click or tap on the Browse button to search your system for the folder storing the file.

Once you specify where the publication is located, the following dialog box will be displayed:

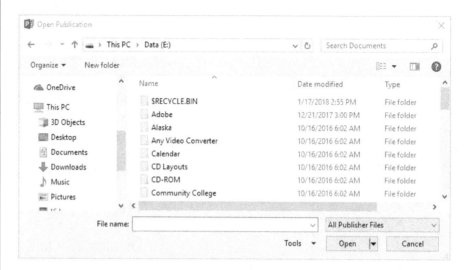

Along the left side of the dialog box, Publisher displays the **Navigation Pane**. This pane lists common/favorite locations (links) as well as a section for browsing your folders and drives.

The address bar is displayed, as shown below:

Notice that the path is displayed horizontally on the bar. For example, in the diagram shown above the currently selected item is the "Data" drive (E) which is part of your computer. To get to that folder, you had to first choose your computer, then the Data drive (E). You could then select the folder containing your Publisher documents.

This layout is commonly referred to as "bread crumbs" because it shows you the path that was taken to get to the current location.

In the example shown on the previous page, you can easily move to another folder on the "E" drive by clicking or tapping on ❯ beside the drive name and then selecting a different folder to view.

Across the top of the window are the following buttons:

Organize ▼   Click or tap this button to access the **Organize** pull-down menu. From the pull-down list, select the operation (e.g., cut, copy, paste, delete, rename) you want to perform on existing files listed within this box.

New folder   Click or tap this button to create a new folder.

When ready, double-click or double-tap on the name of the file you want to open or highlight the name and click or tap ⎣ Open ▼⎦.

| Open |
| Open Read-Only |
| Open in Browser |

If you click or tap on the down arrow ▾ beside the ⎣ Open ▼⎦ button, you can choose to open it as read-only.

| TIP: | *The shortcut key for opening files while working within a publication is* CTRL + O. |

WORKING WITH TEXT

USAGE:

There will be times when you will want to edit existing text within one of your publications. You can change the wording itself, delete it and start over, switch to a different font and point size or apply a number of text attributes.

REPLACING EXISTING TEXT

You can quickly replace a block of existing text using either the mouse or keyboard as discussed below:

Move to the beginning of the text to be selected. Next, click or tap and drag to highlight the desired text.

Move the cursor to the beginning of the text to be selected. Hold the SHIFT key down and use the arrow keys to highlight text.

After you have selected the text (using either the mouse or the keyboard method discussed above), simply begin typing. The highlighted text will be replaced by the new information.

DELETING TEXT

When a block of text is no longer needed, you can remove it and start over.

This key deletes the character to the left of the cursor. Works like a correctable backspace on a typewriter.

This key deletes the current character.

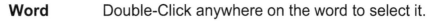

SELECTING TEXT WITH THE MOUSE

You can also use the mouse to quickly select text that you want removed from your publication:

Word   Double-Click anywhere on the word to select it.

Paragraph   Triple-Clicking on a paragraph selects it.

Any Text   Move the Insertion Bar to the beginning of the block you want to delete. Click and drag.

Once the text has been selected, press DEL to remove the block of unwanted text.

OOPS!! UNDELETING TEXT

If you delete an item by mistake, you can undo that deletion. Undo instructs the program to disregard the last action (whether it was deleting, copying, or applying format changes).

↰ ▾   Click or tap on the **UNDO** tool to undo the last action.

If you click or tap on the down arrow ▾ (to the right of the tool), you can scroll through the last several actions. Move your mouse down the list to highlight which actions to undo. They must be done in sequence!

REDOING COMMANDS

If you undo a set of actions and then change your mind (again), you can always "Redo" what you have just undone.

↱   Click or tap on the **REDO** tool to redo the last undo.

APPLYING ATTRIBUTES

As you enter and edit text, you can change its appearance to add emphasis and make the publication easier to read.

The following tools (located on the Home Ribbon) can be used to change the style, font, size, color and attributes of text:

 Click or tap on down arrow ⏷ beside this tool to select a new font.

 Click or tap the down arrow ⏷ beside this tool to select a new font size.

A⁺ A⁻ Use these tools to **increase**/decrease the font size.

B Click or tap this tool to turn **bold** on and off.

I Click or tap this tool to turn *italics* on and off.

U̲ Click or tap this tool to turn underline on and off.

X₂ Click or tap this tool to turn subscript on and off.

x² Click or tap this tool to superscript on and off.

Aa ⏷ Click or tap this tool to specify upper/lower case.

AV ⏷ Use this tool to adjust the spacing between characters.

A ⏷ Click or tap this tool to change the font color.

Aâ To remove unwanted attributes, select the text and then click or tap the **Clear Formatting** tool (located within the Font section on the Home Ribbon).

NOTE: *To change existing text, be sure to select the text first and then choose the desired attribute.*

APPLYING MULTIPLE TEXT FORMATS

To access the more advanced text effects, you will need to access the "Font" dialog box.

Click or tap the **Font Dialog Box Launcher**  (located on the Home Ribbon).

The following dialog box will be displayed:

As you make changes within this dialog box, a preview of your selections is displayed at the bottom.

Font	Scroll through the list of available fonts. They are listed in alphabetical order and contain the fonts currently installed on your system. Simply click on the font you would like to use.
Font style	Scroll through the list of font styles. The styles available will depend on the currently selected font. Click on the style you want to apply.
Font size	Scroll through the list of available font sizes. Simply click on the size you want to apply.
Font color	Click on this box to specify which font color to apply to your text.
	If you want to add special effects (such as a gradient or an outline), click or tap Fill Effects ... to access options for filling your text.
Effects	Use the checkboxes within this section to specify which (if any) effects should be applied to your text. To preview each effect, simply click in its corresponding box (to enable it) and then look at the Preview section (located at the bottom of the dialog box). To remove an unwanted effect, click a second time to remove the check (which will disable the effect).
Underline	Click on this box to specify the type of underline you want to apply to your text.
Typography	Some fonts have additional typography features (such as proportionally spaced numbers or evenly aligning numbers along a baseline). Use this section to adjust the typography to fit your style.
Sample	This section simply displays a preview of the currently selected options within this dialog box to let you see how the text will appear if you accept the current settings.

When done, click or tap OK to accept the changes made within the dialog box and return to your publication.

IDENTIFYING TEXT OVERFLOW

If you have entered more text than can be displayed within the margins of a text box, this icon will be displayed on the border of the box, as a text flow warning. To correct the problem, simply expand the text box.

MOVING OVERFLOW TEXT

If you want to move the overflow text to another text box, follow these steps:

1. Click or tap the button. The mouse pointer will change to

2. Point to the text box in which you want the overflow text to be placed or point to the location where Publisher should create the next text box. Your mouse pointer will change to

3. Click or tap once. Publisher will place the overflow text in the existing text box or will create a new text box.

4. If there is still some overflow text, repeat steps 1-3 as needed.

Linking text boxes can be useful when you need to break up an article across multiple pages. For example, if you're working with a newsletter, you could have the first few paragraphs of an article on the front page and then place the rest of the article as overflow text elsewhere in the newsletter.

The box containing the overflow text will be linked to the original text box. As you add or remove text (from within the original text box), the box containing the overflow text will automatically adjust.

Click or tap ▶ (located on the right border of the original text box) to quickly move to the overflow box. Click on ◀ (located on the left border of the overflow box) to quickly move to the original box. If there are more than two linked text boxes, these arrows will cycle between the previous and next text box.

TEXT AUTOFIT OPTIONS

If you have entered more text than can be displayed within the margins of a text box, you can have Publisher automatically resize the text so that it fits.

Text
Fit ▾

Select the text box and then click or tap this tool (located within the **Text** section on the Text Box Tools Format Ribbon).

The following options are available from the pull-down menu:

Best Fit	Choose this option to have Publisher adjust the font size so that the selected block of text will fit within the current margins of the text box. The font size will continue to be adjusted (increased or decreased) to fit within the margins if the box is resized.
Shrink Text on Overflow	Select this menu item to shrink the font to fit within the current text box margins. If you later shrink the box, the font will continue to be adjusted. However, if you enlarge the box, the text will not increase in size to accommodate the new margins.
Grow Text Box to Fit	Select this menu item to grow the box to fit the text.
Do Not Autofit	If you have already selected one of the other two AutoFit choices from within this submenu, use this option to turn them off.

CHANGING THE COLOR OF THE FONT

Although Publisher defaults to printing your text in black, if you have a color printer you can change the color of the font by accessing the Home Ribbon, as shown in the steps below:

❶ 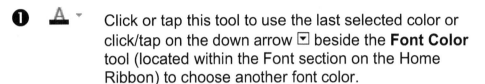 Click or tap this tool to use the last selected color or click/tap on the down arrow ⊡ beside the **Font Color** tool (located within the Font section on the Home Ribbon) to choose another font color.

❷ Select the color you want to use (from the pull-down list) for the selected text.

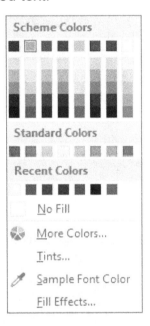

NOTE:	*The color you chose last becomes the default. If you look at the tool, the current color will be shown (as an underline for the letter A on the tool).*

To view the complete color palette, click or tap on 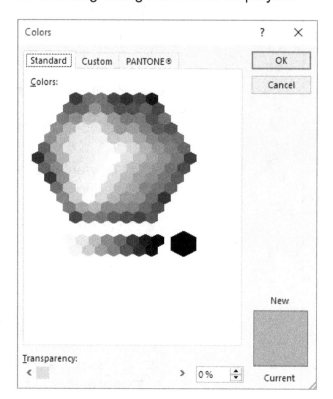 More Colors...

The following dialog box will be displayed:

The first tab (labeled **Standard**) allows you to select from a group of predefined colors.

The box in the lower right corner of the dialog box will display the current font color as well as the new color you select.

The second color tab (labeled **Custom**) allows you to further customize the color applied to the text, as shown below:

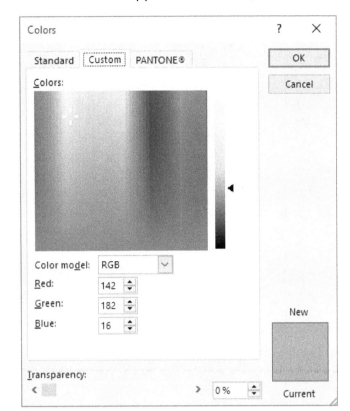

Unless you know the exact values for a particular color, follow the steps shown below to choose a custom color:

❶   Click or tap the palette area on the color to customize. Notice the bottom right corner of the screen contains a box labeled **Current**. Be sure you see the color to customize in that box before continuing to the second step.

❷   Drag the color marker ◄ up or down to intensify the color. Notice the **New** color box at the bottom of the dialog box.

The third tab (labeled **Pantone**) is used for color matching.

The following dialog box will be displayed:

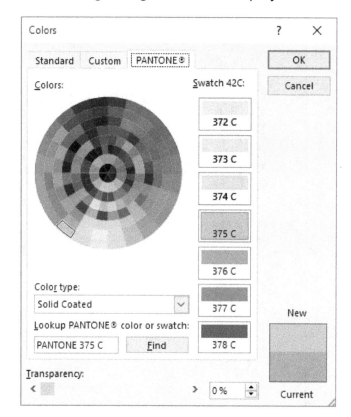

If you are taking your publication to a professional printer, you will want to choose final colors from a color matching system you're your printing service supports. Publisher provides the Pantone Matching System which can be used to specify the spot or process colors to use in your publication.

Notice that Publisher displays a sample of the currently selected color in the bottom right portion of the dialog box.

Once you have chosen the new Pantone color, click or tap OK to close the dialog box and return to your publication.

CHANGING ALIGNMENT

If you are working with a large block of text and would like to alter the alignment of paragraph text, place the cursor anywhere in the paragraph and select one of the alignment tools:

≡   **Left** Aligned

≡   **Centered**

≡   **Right** Aligned

≡   **Full** Justification

INDENTING PARAGRAPHS

You can also indent a block of text. Place the cursor in the paragraph you want to modify and then click on one of these tools to indent/outdent:

⇤≡ ⇥≡   Use these tools to indent/outdent

LINE SPACING

↕≡ ▾   Click or tap on this tool (within the **Paragraph** section of the Home Ribbon) to choose from a list of the most common line spacing settings.

USING THE FORMAT PAINTER

Publisher offers a feature which allows you to copy attributes from one block of text and paste them onto another block within one of your text boxes. This feature can save you time by copying the format of an existing block of text.

To use the format painter, follow the steps outlined below:

❶ Select the text containing the attributes to be copied.

❷   Format Painter   Select the **Format Painter** tool from the Home Ribbon. If you plan on formatting more than one block of text, double-click or double-tap on this tool.

      Your mouse pointer changes to a paintbrush.

❸ Highlight the block of text to be formatted. Publisher will automatically apply the same formatting options you copied. If you only clicked the tool once, Publisher deactivates this feature after the first block is formatted.

❹ If you double-clicked or double-tap the icon to begin with, the Format Painter remains active until you deactivate it by clicking the tool again.

Continue highlighting each block of text to be formatted.

TURNING BULLETS ON

 To include a bullet list within one of your text boxes, click or tap the **Bullet** tool (located on the formatting toolbar). A bullet will precede each new line.

If you had first selected existing text, each selected paragraph will contain bullets.

Move to a blank line and select the bullet tool a second time to turn bullets off from this point on.

TIP: *If you press* ENTER *twice after your last bullet, the bullets will automatically be turned off.*

TURNING NUMBERING ON

To include a numbered list on one of your text boxes, click or tap on the **Numbering** tool (located on the formatting toolbar). A number will precede each new line.

If you had first selected multiple paragraphs, each selected paragraph will be numbered.

Move to a blank line and select the tool a second time to turn numbers off.

TIP: *If you press* ENTER *twice after your last number, the numbering will automatically be turned off.*

USING THE RULER

USAGE:

By default, when you add a text box to your publication, Publisher displays the ruler. This can be helpful for setting tabs and checking margins. If for some reason the ruler disappears, you can display it again by accessing the **View Ribbon** and checking the box labeled **"Rulers"**.

SETTING TABS

When working with text boxes (stories), you might find it useful to create tabs for aligning your text. Tabs are used for creating columnar lists of numbers and text.

In Publisher, you can create four tab types: Left, Center, Right, and Decimal. An example of how text/data lines up under each tab type is listed below:

Left Tab	Center Tab	Right Tab	Decimal Tab
100	100	100	100.00
1000	1000	1000	1000
10	10	10	10.0
1.00	1.00	1.00	100
100.000	100.000	100.000	100.000
10.0	10.0	10.0	10.0
text	text	text	text
more text	more text	more text	more text

The left edge of the ruler contains an icon ⌊ used to select the type of tab or indent required.

⌊ Left Tab

⊥ Center Tab

⌟ Right Tab

⊥ Decimal Tab

To set a tab, follow these two steps:

❶ Choose the appropriate tab style and then move to the position on the ruler where the tab should be inserted.

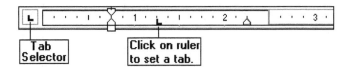

❷ Click the **[LEFT]** mouse button once and the tab will appear.

REMOVING TABS FROM THE RULER

Grab the tab stop and pull it off the ruler.

MOVING A TAB STOP POSITION

Grab the tab stop and drag it to the new location.

WORKING WITH INDENTS

When working with a large text box (story), you might want to indent some of your text. The **left indent** controls the left edge of all lines within a paragraph except the first.

A paragraph's **right indent** controls the right edge of all lines in the paragraph. This indent is measured from the right margin.

A paragraph's **first line indent** controls only the left edge of the paragraph's first line. This indent is measured from the left margin. Setting it to a negative number would create a "hanging indent."

Some examples of indents are shown below:

1. *This is a normal paragraph that has enough text and information to wrap to the full margins of the page.*

      2. *Notice the left edge of this paragraph has been indented to cause the paragraph to be narrower.*

3. *Notice the right edge of this paragraph has been indented to cause the paragraph to be narrower.*

        4. *Notice the first line of this paragraph is "indented" to the right of the body of this paragraph.*

5. *Notice the first line of this paragraph is "hanging" to the left of the body of this paragraph.*

To create the indents, use one of the following options:

    Use the left button to outdent and the right button to indent the current paragraph.

When using the ruler to set indents, drag the indent marker to the desired position.

Notice that when you drag the left indent marker, the first line marker moves with it. This keeps the first line indentation you set as you change the left indent. It is possible to move the first line marker individually.

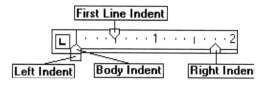

WORKING WITH THE MEASUREMENT TOOLBAR

USAGE:

When working with objects within your publication, you may decide you need to specify precise size dimensions and/or placement. In addition to setting the horizontal and vertical position of an object, its width, height, and rotation angle, you can also specify tracking, scaling, kerning, and line spacing when working with text items.

⊞ 2.82 x 5.10 in.　To view the measurement toolbar, click/tap this tool (located along the left side of the status bar).

Measure... ▼ ✕	
x	0.39"
y	5.75"
width	2.83"
height	2.25"
∠	0°
tracking	100%
scaling	100%
kerning	0 pt

x ▏0.39"▕　Use this box to specify the exact horizontal position for the selected object. Use the arrows along the right side of this box to increase or decrease the current setting.

y ▏5.75"▕　Use this box to specify the exact vertical position for the selected object. Use the arrows along the right side of this box to increase or decrease the current setting.

▏2.83"▕　Use this box to specify the width of the selected object. Use the arrows along the right side of this box to increase or decrease the current setting.

▏2.25"▕　Use this box to specify the height of the selected object. Use the arrows along the right side of this box to increase or decrease the current setting.

∠ ▏0°▕　Use this box to specify the rotation angle for the selected object. Use the arrows along the right side of this box to increase or decrease the current setting.

When working with text objects, the following tools are also available on the measurement toolbar:

ꜣ̣ꜣ̣ꜣ̣ | 100% ↕ | Use this box to specify the tracking position (spacing) between all of the selected text characters. Use the arrows along the right side of this box to increase or decrease the current setting. Notice the font size is not changed - only the spacing between the characters.

↔A→ | 100% ↕ | Use this box to set the scaling. This setting does not change the point size but is used to stretch or shrink the width of each character to make them look very wide or very narrow.

A̅V̅ | 0 pt ↕ | Use this box to specify the kerning (spacing between two text characters). Use the arrows along the right side of this box to increase or decrease the current setting.

✕ When done working with the measurement toolbar, you can remove it from the screen by clicking or tapping on this button (located in the top right corner of the toolbar).

FORMATTING WITH DROP CAPS

USAGE:

When working with a newsletter, you may want to begin new articles by emphasizing the first character of the first word. You can do this by applying a drop cap character.

A drop cap is a special format applied to a character or group of characters to make them stand out from the rest of your text.

To create a drop cap, place your cursor in the paragraph to apply the drop cap to and then click on the following tool:

Click or tap on this tool (located within the **Typography** section on the Text Box Tools Format Ribbon).

From the pull-down list, select the type of drop cap character you wish to apply.

Notice you also have the option of creating your own custom drop cap character. If you choose this last option, the following dialog box will be displayed:

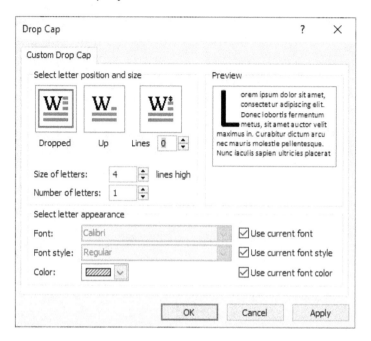

This box contains two main sections, as discussed below:

Select letter position and size   Use this section to define exactly how the drop cap character will be positioned in relation to the rest of the body text, the size of the drop cap letters and the number of letters to be affected.

Select letter appearance   Use this section to specify the font, font style and color to be applied to the drop cap character.

When done, choose OK .

WORKING WITH THE THESAURUS

USAGE:

If you have used a word several times within the same paragraph, you may want to use the thesaurus to look up an alternative word.

You can also use this feature to find a word similar in meaning to the one you want to use but gets the point across a bit stronger.

Thesaurus

Select the word you want to look up and then switch to the Review Ribbon and click on this tool (located within the **Proofing** section) to activate the Thesaurus Task Pane.

A listing of words similar to the one currently selected will be provided within the task pane. If there is more than a screenful, you can move through the list by using the scroll bars provided.

Notice if the selected word has more than one meaning, Publisher displays each of those meanings with a list of alternative words. Each different meaning will have a small triangle to the left, which allows you to display or hide its set of alternative words. The number of meanings will depend on what word is currently selected.

REPLACING A WORD

To replace the word in your publication with one of the choices provided within the task pane, simply point and then click or tap on the down arrow ▾ (which only appears when you point to a word) beside the new word and choose **Insert** from the pop-up list provided.

Notice you can also copy the word to paste in another location or lookup the selected word.

LOOKING UP A NEW WORD

To look up a different word, simply click or tap in the box labeled **Search** and then enter the new word. After entering the word, either press ENTER or click on 🔎 .

If you have looked up more than one word, click or tap on ❮ to return to the previous listing.

INSERTING THE DATE & TIME

USAGE:

You can quickly insert the current date and time into one of your text boxes. In addition to selecting the exact format for the date/time, you can also specify whether it should be updated automatically. This can be useful for newsletters you create on a monthly basis.

Date & Time

Select a text object and then click or tap on this tool (located within the **Text** section of the Insert Ribbon).

The following dialog box will be displayed:

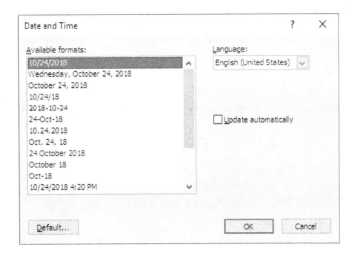

Click or tap Default... to change the default setting within Publisher to the currently selected format. This setting will be used for any date codes added to this or future publications.

Check the box labeled **Update automatically** to have the date automatically updated to the current date/time whenever you open the publication.

Select the desired format and choose OK.

ADDING SYMBOLS

USAGE:

In addition to letters, numbers and punctuation, you can insert special symbols as bullets into your publication. You may also access a special character to add a business symbol (such as a trademark character). You can access these symbols by switching to another font and then selecting the key representing the symbol.

To insert a symbol or special character, follow the steps below:

❶ Place your cursor at the location within a text box where you want to insert the symbol or special character and then click on this tool (located within the **Text** section on the Insert Ribbon).

❷  From the pull-down list, select the symbol you'd like to insert.

If you selected "More Symbols…" from the pull-down list, the following dialog box will be displayed:

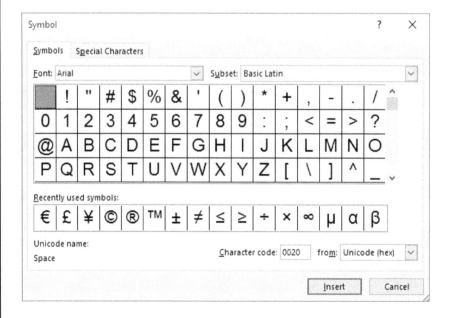

To insert a symbol, select the **Symbols** tab. To insert a special character, select the tab labeled **Special Characters**. When working with symbols, click on any of the symbols in the box to see an enlarged view of it.

Font   Click or tap on the down arrow 🔽 to select the font containing the symbol you want to insert. There are special font sets that can contain different types of symbols/characters.

Subset   Click or tap on the down arrow 🔽 beside this box to choose an actual set of characters available with the selected font. For example, if you were looking for the British Pound sign, you would choose "Currency Symbols" as the subset in order to locate that symbol.

Insert   Click or tap on this button to actually insert the symbol into your publication.

Once the symbol has been inserted, click or tap Close to close the dialog box and return to your publication.

MOVING OBJECTS

USAGE:

You can move any object (such as one of your text boxes) around within your publication by dragging them from one location to another using your mouse, as outlined in the steps shown below.

❶   Move to the middle of the selected item.

Be sure the mouse pointer changes to the four-way arrow. Click and drag the object to its new location.

❷   Once you reach the new location, release the mouse button and the original object will appear in its new location.

If you need to move an item from one page to another, it's easier to cut and paste the item, as shown in the steps below:

❶   Select the item to be moved.

❷   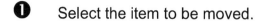 Cut   Click or tap the **Cut** tool (which is located on the Home Ribbon). The object is temporarily removed from the screen and placed in the clipboard.

❸   Move to the new location.

❹   Click or tap on the top half of the **Paste** tool.

Paste

   If you click on the bottom half of the Paste tool, a pull-down list appears, which provides additional paste options (such as merging the original format with the current location's format or pasting only the text, without any of its original formatting).

Once an item is pasted, a small clipboard icon will be added to your screen (Ctrl) ▾ (which offers the same list of options from the Paste pull-down list).

COPYING OBJECTS

USAGE:

To copy an object to another location within your publication, follow these steps:

❶ Move to the middle of the object. Be sure that the mouse pointer changes to the four-way arrow.

Hold down the **CTRL** key. You'll see a small plus symbol (**+**) on the mouse pointer. Continue to hold the **CTRL** key down while dragging the object to its new location.

❷ Once you reach your destination, release the mouse button and then the **CTRL** key. The original object will be copied to its new location.

To copy an object to another page within your publication, follow these steps:

❶ Select the object to be copied.

❷ 🗎 Copy   Click or tap the **Copy** tool (which is located on the Home Ribbon). The object is temporarily copied to the clipboard.

❸ Move to the new location.

❹ Click or tap on the top half of the **Paste** tool.

Paste

Paste Options:

Paste Special...

If you click on the bottom half of the Paste tool, a pull-down list appears, which provides additional paste options (such as merging the original format with the current location's format or pasting only the text, without any of its original formatting).

Once an item is pasted, a small clipboard icon will be added to your screen 🗎 (Ctrl) ▾ (which offers the same list of options from the Paste pull-down list).

USING THE OFFICE CLIPBOARD

USAGE:

You can use the Office Clipboard to collect multiple items (both text and graphics) to be pasted within Publisher or other Office applications. The standard Windows clipboard is only able to store one item at a time. You have to paste whatever you have cut or copied before your next cut/copy can be completed.

However, the Office Clipboard can store up to 24 items at a time, making it easy to collect multiple items to be pasted. If you copy a 25th item, the first item in your clipboard will automatically be removed to make room for the latest entry.

Depending on your computer's settings, choosing to copy an item and then copying a second one without pasting the first may trigger the Clipboard task pane to be displayed.

If the task pane is not automatically displayed, you can manually display it by accessing the following tool:

Click or tap the **Clipboard Task Pane Launcher** ⌐▪ (located along the far left side of the Home Ribbon).

The Office Clipboard will automatically be opened and placed within a task pane, as shown below:

The clipboard will display each of the cut or copied items - with the latest item placed at the top of the list. If you have cut or copied several entries, a scroll bar will be placed along the right side so that you can quickly move through the items.

A small icon is placed to the left of each object to indicate what application the cut or copied item was originally created in.

Move to the location to which the item(s) should be pasted.

Click or tap on the clipboard item to be pasted.

There are two tools available across the top of the clipboard:

Paste All	Click or tap this tool to paste each of the items stored within the Office Clipboard in the current publication (or within the current Office application).
Clear All	Click or tap this button to clear the contents of the Office Clipboard. It will also clear the Windows Clipboard.

To remove a single item from the clipboard, point to the item you want to remove until you see a small down arrow ⏷.

Click or tap the down arrow ⏷ and select **Delete** from the list of options.

CLIPBOARD OPTIONS

Towards the bottom of the clipboard is a button Options which is used to change the display settings for the Office Clipboard.

Show Office Clipboard Automatically

Show Office Clipboard When Ctrl+C Pressed Twice

Collect Without Showing Office Clipboard

✓ Show Office Clipboard Icon on Taskbar

✓ Show Status Near Taskbar When Copying

From the five options available, check the box labeled **Show Office Clipboard Automatically** to open the clipboard within the task pane when two items in a row have been copied.

Select **Show Office Clipboard When Ctrl+C Pressed Twice** to display the Office Clipboard after pressing the copy shortcut keys.

Choose **Collect Without Showing Office Clipboard** if you prefer not to display the clipboard within the task pane when two items in a row have been copied. This option displays the clipboard icon on the taskbar even if you are in a different application. Make sure the first two options have not been checked.

Select **Show Office Clipboard Icon on Taskbar** to display the clipboard icon at the bottom of your screen.

Choose **Show Status Near Taskbar When Copying** to display the status of a copied item on the taskbar.

Check each of the options you would like to enable from the list. Click a second time to disable the option.

Once the Office Clipboard has been activated, an icon will be placed on the Windows taskbar (notification tray) along the bottom right of your screen.

If you don't see the Office Clipboard icon on your taskbar, it may be one of the hidden items. Click on ⌃ to view the hidden items.

If you right-click or tap and hold (if using a touch screen) on the clipboard icon located along the taskbar at the bottom of your screen, the following list of options will be displayed:

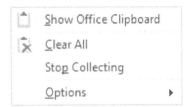

From this list, you can choose to display the Office Clipboard, clear all of the items currently being stored within the clipboard, or close the clipboard. The last item within this list allows you to specify the display options for the clipboard (which were discussed on the previous page).

If you do not specify otherwise, the collected items remain in the Clipboard until you close all Office applications.

RESIZING OBJECTS

USAGE:

You can easily change an object's size - keeping its original proportions or changing its shape as you resize.

To resize an object, follow the steps outlined below:

 ❶ ⇔↕↖↗ Move the mouse so the tip of the arrow touches one of the surrounding handles. The pointer will change to one of these double-sided arrows.

❷ Use one of the four corner handles to change the object's height and width at the same time.

❸ When done, release the button

NOTE:	Dragging the handles of a text box only serves to change the left or right margins of the text block. This may cause the text to wrap within the margins.

DELETING OBJECTS

USAGE:

There may be times while editing a publication that you decide that an object is no longer needed and should be removed entirely. Rather than deleting the text within a text box, you may decide you want the entire text box itself removed from your publication.

To remove any object from your publication, follow these steps:

❶   Select the object(s) to be deleted.

❷   Press the ⌊DEL⌋ key and the object(s) will be removed.

OOPS! UNDELETING

If you mistakenly delete an object from your publication, you can undo the deletion, as shown below:

↶▾   Click or tap on this tool (located on Quick Access toolbar) to **Undo** the last action. To undo more than one action, click on the down arrow ▾ beside the tool

ROTATING OBJECTS

USAGE:

Publisher makes it easy for you to position objects in the exact angle you need.

To rotate an object, follow these steps:

❶ Select the object to be rotated.

❷
Rotate

Click or tap on the down arrow ⊡ beside this tool (located within the **Arrange** section of the Drawing Tools Format Ribbon).

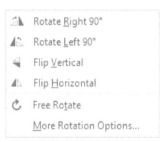

From the pull-down list, select the rotation angle for the selected item.

Rotate Right 90°	Select this option to quickly rotate the selected object 90 degrees to the right.
Rotate Left 90°	Choose this option to quickly rotate the selected object 90 degrees to the left.
Flip Vertical	Select this option to quickly flip the selected object vertically.
Flip Horizontal	Choose this item to flip the selected object horizontally.
Free Rotate	Select this option to rotate the object yourself. If for some reason you did not see the rotate handle on the object, you can select this option to display it and then rotate the object yourself.
More Rotation Options…	Select this option to access a dialog box where you can specify an exact rotation angle.

You can rotate an object using the mouse by following these steps:

❶ Select the object you want to rotate.

❷ 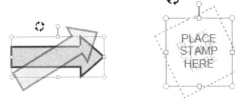 Select the small circle on the rotation handle (which is automatically displayed above the selected object). If using a mouse, the pointer will change to a rotation icon (↻).

❸ Begin dragging clockwise or counter-clockwise to rotate the selected object. As you drag, the mouse pointer will change shape again (↻).

❹ When you are finished, let go of the mouse button (or your finger if working with a touch screen) and the object will be redrawn in its new position

WORKING WITH LAYERS

USAGE:

If you have placed several objects on your page, you may find that one is overlapping another. Since graphic objects can be placed anywhere within a publication, they can at times be placed on top of each other - thereby overlapping. This can be used to combine several layers of objects to create special effects or even a new picture.

For example, the illustration below started out with a picture of a dog carrying a newspaper. The text was then added and placed on top of the newspaper.

To do this, you would simply add the text within a text box and then drag the text box on top of the dog picture.

However, you may find that when you drag one object on top of another they are overlapped incorrectly, as shown below:

BRINGING AN OBJECT FORWARD

To bring an object forward, follow these steps:

❶ Select the object to be placed on top of the other(s).

❷  Click or tap the down arrow ⊡ beside this tool (located within the **Arrange** section of the Home Ribbon) to choose whether the selected object should be brought forward one position (layer) or brought to the front of all objects it shares space with.

SENDING AN OBJECT BACK

To send an object back, follow these steps:

❶ Select the object to be placed behind the other(s).

❷ Send Backward ▾ Click or tap on the down arrow ⊡ beside this tool (located within the **Arrange** section of the Home Ribbon) to choose whether the selected object should be sent back one position (layer) at a time. If you have more than two objects overlapping, you may want the selected item sent behind all others.

PRACTICE EXERCISE

Instructions:

❶ Open the brochure you created during the last module.

❷ Apply a new background to the publication.

❸ Select one of the text boxes (stories) and edit it.

❹ Format the first character of the text box you just edited to have a drop cap character. Choose whatever style you wish for the drop cap character.

❺ Insert the current date & time in one of your text boxes and make sure it is updated automatically whenever the brochure is edited.

❻ Open the flyer publication you created during the last module and then copy one of the objects from that publication to your brochure.

❼ Resize and rotate the copied object.

❽ Close and save both publications.

Module Four

- **Working with Online Pictures**
- **Adding & Customizing Graphics**
- **Inserting AutoShapes**
- **Working with Tables**
- **Adding WordArt**
- **Adding a Design Gallery Object**

WORKING WITH ONLINE PICTURES

USAGE:

Online pictures are ready-made drawings which can be added to your publication. Publisher comes with several hundred pictures, videos and sounds to choose from.

INSERTING AN ONLINE PICTURE

To insert an online picture, follow the steps outlined below:

❶   Click or tap on the **Online Pictures** tool (located within the **Illustrations** section of the Insert Ribbon).

Online Pictures

A window displays categories of available clip art to choose from, as shown below:

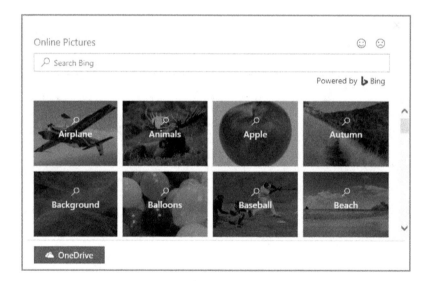

❷   In the box provided, select a category or type in the keyword(s) that best defines what type of picture you are looking for.

Publisher will search through its libraries and online to locate pictures that best match the search criteria you have entered and display them for you, as shown below:

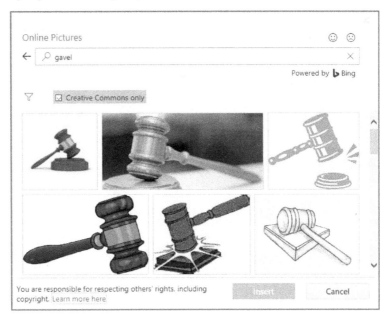

By default, Bing displays pictures it 'assumes' are free to use. However, you are still responsible for ensuring you have permission to use the selected picture.

❸   Select the picture(s) you want to insert into your publication and then click or tap on the   Insert   button.

Once the picture has been placed on the publication, you can manipulate it (e.g., change its size and placement) just as you would any other drawing object.

REMOVING AN ONLINE PICTURE

To remove a picture from your publication, follow the two steps outlined below:

❶   Click or tap on the picture to select it.

❷   Press

ADDING TEXT AND GRAPHIC OBJECTS

USAGE:

If you cannot find an online picture that depicts the exact drawing you want in your publication, use Publisher's drawing tools to create your own logos or other graphics. You can also add additional text boxes when needed.

To create a text box, follow these steps:

❶

Draw
Text Box

Select the text box tool (located within the **Objects** section on the Home Ribbon).

❷ Move to the location where the text box should be inserted. Click and drag to define the size and placement of the text box. When you release the mouse button, the text box will appear.

❸ You'll see your cursor blinking in the box, indicating you are ready to begin entering text.

You can use all of the same formatting tools to change the font, size, color, and apply attributes (such as bold, italics) to text box data that you would to any other text stored within your publication.

> **NOTE:** *If you do not click and drag (as defined in Step 2), and simply click once, Publisher will insert a default 1" text box at the location where you clicked. If you type more text than fits within the box, you will need to resize the box to accommodate the extra text.*

ADDING SHAPES

To add a shape to the current publication, follow these steps:

❶ Click or tap on this tool (located within the **Objects** section of the Home Ribbon).

❷ 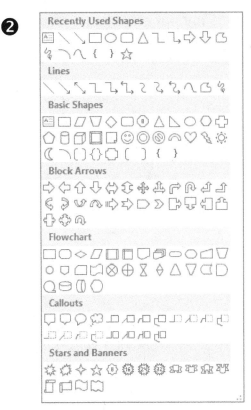 From the pull-down list select the shape you want to create.

❸ Position the cross-hair pointer where the top left corner of the shape should begin.

❹ Drag to the size and position where the bottom right corner of the shape should appear.

❺ Release the mouse button (or your finger if working on a touch screen device) when you are done drawing.

ADJUSTING SHAPES

Many of the AutoShapes have an extra adjustment handle in the shape of a yellow diamond (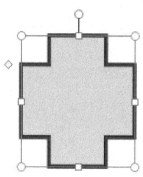).

You can use this to adjust some aspect of the shape such as the thickness of an arrowhead or the roundness of the corners of a rectangle. This adjustment handle is not used to change the size of the shape but rather the most prominent feature of the shape.

The exact adjustment feature will depend on the selected shape.

To adjust the shape, follow the steps outlined below:

❶   Place the mouse pointer over the yellow adjustment handle. The mouse pointer will change to a smaller arrow ( ).

❷   Drag the handle in the direction you want. You will see an outline of the new shape to help you decide when to stop.

❸   Once the adjustment is made, release the mouse button.

ATTACHING TEXT TO A SHAPE

 Edit Text To add text to a shape, select the shape and then click or tap this tool (located within the **Insert Shapes** on the Drawing Tools Format Ribbon).

> **TIP:** *You can also attach text to a shape by simply selecting the shape and then begin typing.*

You can change the font, size, color, and any other text attributes just as you would any other text within your publication. Select the text and then choose the font/size/attribute from the **Font** section of the Home Ribbon.

When you select a block of text, Publisher displays a small toolbar. This small toolbar helps you work with fonts, font styles, font sizing, alignment, text color, indent levels, and bullet features.

When you see the small toolbar appear, simply point to the attribute you want to set and select it with your mouse.

ALIGNING TEXT WITHIN A SHAPE

When you add text to a shape, Publisher automatically aligns it along the left side. To change the alignment, place your cursor anywhere within the text and select one of the following tools (located on the **Home Ribbon**):

Left Aligned

Centered

Right Aligned

Full Justification

EDITING A SHAPE

If you have added a shape which you now need to edit, click or tap this tool (located within the **Insert Shapes** section of the Drawing Tools Format Ribbon) and choose the item you wish to edit (the shape's points, the text wrapping points or the shape's connectors). Not all options are available for every shape.

CHANGING A SHAPE

 Change Shape ▾

If you decide you added the wrong shape to your publication, select the current shape and then click or tap this tool (located within the **Insert Shapes** section of the Drawing Tools Format Ribbon) and choose a new shape.

ADJUSTING A SHAPE STYLE

You can quickly change the style of a shape by selecting it and then choosing one of these styles.

DEFINING HOW TEXT WRAPS AROUND OBJECTS

Wrap Text ▾

Click or tap this tool (located within the **Arrange** section of the Home Ribbon or the Drawing Tools Format Ribbon) to define how text will wrap around a shape (or any other graphic object). You can choose to have no text wrapping, a square space around the shape, have text tightly wrapped around the shape, only have text above or below the shape (no text on either side), or choose **Through** if you want to edit text wrapping points.

REMOVING A SHAPE

If you decide you no longer want the shape you can easily remove it by selecting the shape and pressing the DEL key.

CUSTOMIZING OBJECTS

USAGE:

Once an item has been placed within your publication, you may want to customize its appearance. You can align multiple objects, change the color of the lines surrounding an object or its fill pattern, add shading or even apply special effects to some objects.

ALIGNING MULTIPLE OBJECTS

Publisher allows you to align multiple items within a publication. For example, you may want the tops of each selected object to line up or the center point of each object to be aligned. You can also choose to align them evenly on the page.

❶   Select each of the objects you want to align.

❷      Click or tap on the down arrow ⌄ beside one of these tools (located within the **Arrange** section of the Home Ribbon or the Drawing Tools Format Ribbon) to specify the alignment.

❸   From the pull-down list, choose the alignment option you wish to set for the selected objects.

GROUPING MULTIPLE OBJECTS

Sometimes you will want to group a set of objects so that you can move or edit them as a single item. This can make editing much faster (i.e., changing outline styles, colors, etc.).

❶   Select the objects to be grouped as one item by holding `CTRL` and clicking on each item.

❷   ⊞ Group   Click or tap this tool (located within the **Arrange** section of the Home Ribbon) to group each of the selected objects.

         ⊟ Ungroup   Once grouped, click or tap this tool if you decide grouping the items was a mistake and you now want to ungroup them.

COMPRESSING PICTURES

 Compress Pictures

If you decide you would like to reduce the size of your document by compressing the pictures stored in it, simply select the picture and then click or tap this tool (located within the **Adjust** section on the Picture Tools Format Ribbon). Publisher will provide several options for compressing the picture(s), as well as a recap of the final picture size after compression. You can choose to compress all pictures within the presentation or just the selected picture(s).

CHANGING A PICTURE

Change Picture ▾

Choose this tool (located within the **Adjust** section on the Picture Tools Format Ribbon) to change the selected image.

From the pull-down menu, choose whether you want to change the picture or remove it.

RESIZING AN OBJECT

Use these two sections (located within the **Adjust** section on the Picture Tools Format Ribbon to specify an exact height and width for the graphic object.

RESETTING AN OBJECT

Reset Picture

If you decide you have made changes to the object that you don't want to save, click or tap this tool (located within the **Adjust** section on the Picture Tools Format Ribbon) to reset the object to its original properties.

CHANGING OUTLINE/LINE COLOR AND STYLE

To modify the color or line style applied to the outline of a shape or a text box, follow the steps below:

❶   Select the object to be modified.

❷      Click or tap this tool (located within the **Shape Styles** section on the Drawing Tools Format Ribbon).

❸   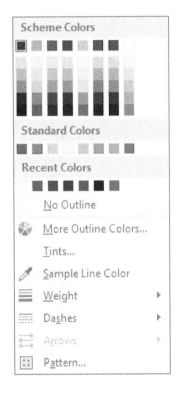   From this pull-down list, you can choose a new outline color, remove the outline altogether, change the weight of the outline, and change the style of the line to include dashes, arrows, or a pattern.

If you do not see the desired color from the list, select **More Outline Colors...** which displays the entire color palette.

Notice as you move your mouse over each color within the list, a preview is provided of the selected object using the color you are currently pointing to.

CHANGING FILL COLORS

To modify the fill color, picture, gradient, and texture applied to a shape or text box, follow the steps outlined below:

❶   Select the object to be modified.

❷   

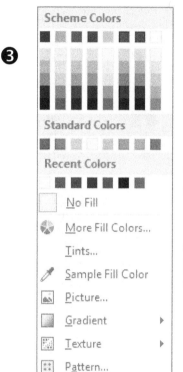

Click or tap on this tool (located within the **Shape Styles** section on the Drawing Tools Format Ribbon).

❸

From this pull-down list, you can choose a new fill color, remove the fill altogether, or change the fill to include a picture, a gradient, texture, or pattern.

If you do not see the desired color from the list, select **More Fill Colors...** which displays the entire color palette.

Notice as you move your mouse over each color within the list, a preview is provided of the selected object using the color you are currently pointing to.

A gradient typically consists of two colors gradually blending from one color to the other. You can select the colors to be used as well as the intensity and the direction in which the gradient will be generated.

Textures are basically small patches of patterns that resemble real-life textures such as marble, cloth, grass, paper, wood, etc.

Rather than using a color or one of the built-in textures or patterns, you can fill an object with a custom picture. Publisher recognizes most graphic file formats to provide you with a wide variety of options.

ADDING A SHADOW

You can also apply a shadow effect to a shape or text box by following the steps shown below:

❶ Select the object(s) to modify.

❷  Click or tap this button (located within the **Shape Styles** section on the Drawing Tools Format Ribbon).

❸ From the pull-down list, select **Shadow** and then choose the type of shadow effect to apply to the selected object.

ADDING A 3-D EFFECT

You can also apply 3-D effects to shapes and text boxes by following the steps shown below:

❶ Select the object to modify.

❷  Click or tap this button (located within the **Shape Effects** section on the Drawing Tools Format Ribbon).

❸ From the pull-down list, select **3-D Rotation** and then the type of 3-D effect to apply to the selected object.

WORKING WITH WORDART

USAGE:

Publisher offers a feature which allows you to create text objects that use fancy special effects. This can greatly enhance your publication and make it appear much more professional.

To insert a WordArt object, follow these steps:

❶ WordArt

Click or tap this tool (located within the **Text** section of the Insert Ribbon) to add a WordArt object to your publication.

A pull-down list will appear displaying the various styles of WordArt, as shown below:

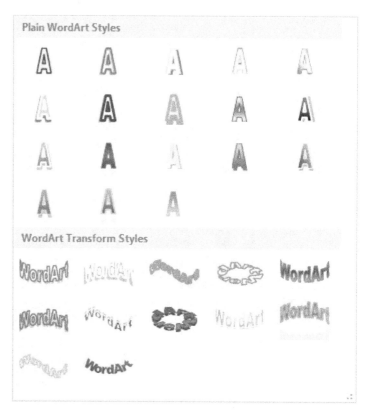

❷ From the pull-down list, select the style to apply.

A dialog box will be opened where you can the actual text:

❸ Enter the text within the box provided. When done, click or tap OK . Your WordArt object will be displayed:

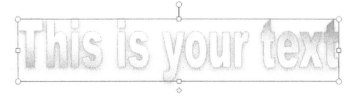

CHANGING OUTLINE COLOR AND STYLE

To modify the color applied to the outline surrounding the WordArt object as well as the style of the outline, follow the steps below:

❶ Select the WordArt object.

❷ 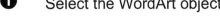 Click or tap this button (located within the **WordArt Styles** section of the WordArt Tools Format Ribbon).

❸  From this pull-down list, you can choose a new outline color, remove the outline altogether, change the weight of the outline, and change the style of the line to include dashes or arrows.

If you do not see the desired color from the list, select **More Outline Colors...** which displays the entire color palette.

CHANGING FILL COLORS

To modify the fill color, picture, gradient, and texture applied to the box surrounding a WordArt object, follow the steps outlined below:

❶   Select the WordArt object to be modified.

❷   Shape Fill ▾   Click or tap this button (located within the **WordArt Styles** section on the WordArt Tools Format Ribbon).

❸

From this pull-down list, you can choose a new fill color, remove the fill altogether, or change the fill to include a picture, a gradient, or a texture.

If you do not see the desired color from the list, select **More Fill Colors...** which displays the entire color palette.

Notice as you move your mouse over each of the options within the list, Publisher provides a preview of the selected WordArt object using the option you are currently pointing to.

A gradient typically consists of two colors gradually blending from one color to the other. You can select the colors to be used as well as the intensity and the direction in which the gradient will be generated. Textures are basically small patches of patterns that resemble real-life textures such as marble, cloth, grass, paper, wood, etc. Patterns use geometric patterns to fill the WordArt object. Rather than using one of the built-in textures or patterns, you can choose to fill a WordArt object with a custom picture. Publisher recognizes most graphic file formats to provide you with a wide variety of options

ADDING A SHAPE EFFECT

Adding a shape effect (such as a shadow or a bevel effect) can give the WordArt object a more custom look and feel to help it to stand out from the rest of the drawing.

To apply a shape effect to a WordArt object, follow these steps:

❶ Select the WordArt object to be modified.

❷  Click or tap this button (located within the **WordArt Styles** section on the WordArt Tools Format Ribbon).

❸  From this pull-down list, choose the shape effect you wish to apply to the selected object.

Notice as you move your mouse over each of the options within the list, Publisher provides a preview of the selected WordArt object using the option you are currently pointing to.

CHANGING THE WORDART SHAPE

To change the shape of the WordArt object, follow these steps:

❶ Select the WordArt object to be modified.

❷ Click or tap this tool (located within the **WordArt Styles** section of the WordArt Tools Format Ribbon).

❸ 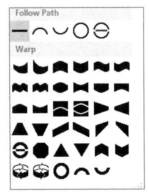 From this pull-down, select the new shape for the WordArt object.

EDITING WORDART TEXT

To modify the text itself, follow these steps:

❶ Select the WordArt object to be modified.

❷ 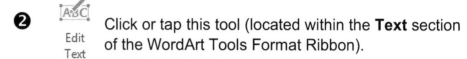 Click or tap this tool (located within the **Text** section of the WordArt Tools Format Ribbon).

❸ The original text box will be displayed once again for you to edit the text within the WordArt object.

❹ When done, click or tap 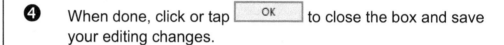 to close the box and save your editing changes.

ADJUSTING CHARACTER SPACING

To change the spacing between characters within the WordArt object, follow these steps:

❶ Select the WordArt object to be modified.

❷ Click or tap this tool (located within the **Text** section of the WordArt Tools Format Ribbon).

❸ 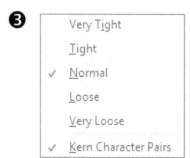 From this pull-down list, choose the character spacing you'd like applied to the WordArt object. Tight is very close together while loose keeps characters further apart.

ADDITIONAL MODIFICATIONS

To modify the height and vertical alignment between characters within the WordArt object, follow these steps:

❶ Select the WordArt object to be modified.

❷  Use these tools (located within the **Text** section of the WordArt Tools Format Ribbon) to modify height.

The first tool ensures all characters are the exact same height. The second tool draws text vertically with letters stacked on top of one another while the last tool specifies how individual lines of a multi-line WordArt object should be aligned.

APPLYING A NEW STYLE TO A WORDART OBJECT

If you realize you selected a style that doesn't work for the WordArt object you are creating, you can quickly choose another shape by following the steps outlined below:

❶ Select the WordArt object to be modified.

❷

Choose from one of the styles listed within the box shown above (located within the **WordArt Styles** section on the WordArt Tools Format Ribbon). Click or tap on ⊟ to display all of the available styles within a single box.

WORKING WITH TABLES

USAGE:

At some point, you will probably create a publication that includes columns and rows of data. Instead of trying to line the data up manually, you can insert something called a **table**.

The structure of a table consists of rows (which run horizontally) and columns (which run vertically). The intersections between these rows and columns are referred to as **cells**. These cells are where you will store your text/images.

To create a table, follow these steps:

 Move to the location where you want to insert the new table and then click or tap this tool (located within the **Tables** section on the Insert Ribbon).

Table

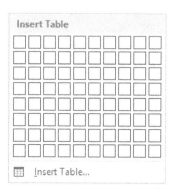

Highlight the number of rows and columns you need and then click the **[LEFT]** mouse button to insert the table into the publication.

If you prefer to manually enter the number of columns and rows, you can select **Insert Table...** from the pull-down list. The following dialog box will be displayed:

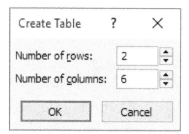

Enter the number of columns and rows required for the table in the boxes provided. When done, choose OK .

The following movement keys may be used within tables:

TAB	Moves to the next cell
SHIFT + TAB	Moves to the previous cell

TIP:	*If you are in the last cell of the last row, pressing* TAB *will create a new row for you.*

HIDING/DISPLAYING THE GRIDLINES

You can choose to display or hide the gridlines, depending on your preference.

View
Gridlines

Click or tap this tool (located within the **Table** section on the Table Tools Layout Ribbon) to toggle gridlines on/off.

LAYOUT RIBBON TOOLS

The Layout Ribbon contains a variety of arrangement tools:

Wrap Text ▾

Click or tap this tool to define how text should wrap around the table.

Bring Forward ▾

Click or tap this tool to bring the selected table in front of any other objects it shares space with.

Send Backward ▾

Click or tap on this tool to send the table behind other objects it shares space with.

Align ▾

Use this tool to align the table with other selected objects on the screen.

 Group

Click or tap this tool to group the table with any other objects currently selected.

 Ungroup

Once grouped, select this tool to ungroup the table from other objects.

Rotate ▾

Use this tool to rotate the table.

The Table Tools Layout Ribbon also includes three sizing tools:

 Height: 2.75"

Use this tool to change the height of the table.

▭ Width: 4.97"

Use this tool to change the width of the table.

☑ Grow to Fit Text

Check this box to allow the table to grow as text is added.

CHANGING THE COLUMN WIDTH

You can change the width of a single column or a group of columns within Publisher's table feature.

To select a column, point just outside the upper table border above the column you want to select. When the pointer changes to a down arrow ⬇ , click or tap to select the current column. To select more than one column, click or tap and drag to highlight each column.

Once the column(s) has been selected, move the mouse pointer to the right edge of the column (in the table itself) until it changes to a double-sided arrow.

 When you see the double arrow, use your mouse to click and drag the column border left/right to its new width. When done, release the mouse button. If more than one column was selected, they will all be the same size.

CHANGING THE ROW HEIGHT

You can also change the height of a single row or a group of rows within the table.

To select a row, point just outside the left table border of the row you want to select. When the pointer changes to an arrow ➡, click or tap to select the current row. To select more than one row, click or tap and drag to highlight each row.

To change the row height, follow the steps shown below:

 ❶ Place the mouse pointer on the bottom gridline of the row you want to adjust. A double arrow will appear. Drag up or down to adjust the row's height.

❷ When the desired height is reached, release the mouse button and the row will adjust to its new height. If more than one row was selected, they will all be the same size.

APPLYING CHARACTER AND PARAGRAPH ATTRIBUTES

The Home Ribbon can be accessed as always to center the contents within a cell or to apply an attribute (e.g., different font, point size, apply bold, etc.). Select the cell(s) to be affected and then click or tap on the appropriate tool.

CHANGING THE TEXT DIRECTION

While working within a table, you might want to change the direction of the text so that it reads sideways going up or down.

Text Direction

To change the direction of text within a cell, select the cell(s) to be adjusted and then click or tap this tool (located within the **Alignment** section of the Table Tools Layout Ribbon). Notice that each time you click or tap on this tool, the direction is changed.

CHANGING THE ALIGNMENT

You can also change the alignment of data within a cell or group of cells by clicking or tapping one of these tools (located within the **Alignment** section of the Table Tools Layout Ribbon).

Most of these options are only noticeable if the cell height/width is much larger than its contents.

CHANGING CELL MARGINS

To adjust the cell margins and the spacing between cells for your table:

Click or tap this tool (located within the **Alignment** section of the Table Tools Layout Ribbon).

Choose your margins from the list of pre-defined settings.

If you need different margins than those provided, click/tap on **"Custom Margins..."**

A dialog box will be displayed.

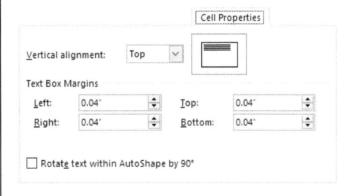

In the boxes provided, select the top, bottom, left, and right margins for each cell.

In addition, there's a checkbox to automatically adjust the cell size to accommodate the contents of the cell.

Once you've made your selection, choose .

INSERTING A COLUMN/ROW

Once you have created a table, you may want to add a column/row to it. To insert a new column or row, follow the steps below:

❶   Click or tap within the column or row where you want the new column/row inserted and then switch to your Table Tools Layout Ribbon.

❷   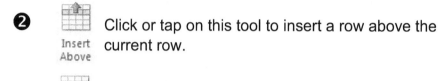 Click or tap on this tool to insert a row above the current row.

Use this tool to insert a row below the current row.

Click or tap on this tool to insert a column to the left of the current column.

Use this tool to insert a column to the right of the current column.

If you select more than one column or row and then click or tap on the table tool, Publisher will assume you want to insert as many rows/columns as you have selected.

DELETING COLUMNS/ROWS

To remove an unwanted column or row, follow these steps:

❶   Select the column(s) or row(s) to be removed.

❷   Click or tap this tool (located on the Table Tools Layout Ribbon) and then select what it is you want to delete from the pull-down list.

Notice you can choose to delete the currently selected column(s), row(s) or the entire table.

MERGING CELLS

If you wish to combine two or more adjacent cells into a single one, follow these steps:

❶   Select the cells to be merged.

❷   Click or tap this tool (located within the **Merge** section on the Table Tools Layout Ribbon) to merge the selected cells into one cell.

Merge Cells

SPLITTING CELLS

If you have a merged two or more adjacent cells and then changed your mind, you can split them again by following the steps below:

❶   Select the cell that was merged but should now be split.

❷   Click or tap this tool (located within the **Merge** section on the Table Tools Layout Ribbon).

Split Cells

PLACING BORDERS AROUND THE TABLE

Each cell can have a different set of borders allowing you to create a variety of table formats.

Follow these three steps to add a border to a cell or group of cells:

❶ Select the cell(s) you want to format.

❷ ⊞ Borders ▾   Click or tap on the down arrow ⊡ beside this tool (located within the **Border** section on the Table Tools Design Ribbon) to select the type of border to apply.

A pull-down list of the available borders is displayed:

⊞	Bottom Border
⊞	Top Border
⊞	Left Border
⊞	Right Border
⊞	No Border
⊞	All Borders
⊞	Outside Borders
⊞	Inside Borders
⊞	Inside Horizontal Border
⊞	Inside Vertical Border
⊠	Diagonal Borders

❸ From the list provided, choose the type of border you would like to apply to the selected cell(s).

USING TABLE FORMATS

You can further customize your table by selecting from one of the many predefined table formats available within Publisher.

To apply one of these formats, follow these steps:

❶   Select the table by clicking or tapping on any of the cells within it.

❷   Use the section shown below (located within the **Table Formats** section on the Table Tools Design Ribbon) to choose a different format for the table.

Notice as you move the mouse pointer over the various formats within the list, your table will change to display a preview of what it will look like if you select that style.

Use the ⬍ buttons to scroll up and down through the list of available formats.

Click on ⬇ to display the entire list of table formats within a single pull-down list.

MOVING A TABLE

Like any other object within a publication, a table can be moved or resized.

To move the table, point to one of the borders surrounding it until you see the mouse pointer change to four-way arrow and then click and drag it to a new location.

DELETING A TABLE

To remove a table from your publication, click or tap this tool (located within the **Rows & Columns** section on the Table Tools Layout Ribbon).

From the pull-down list, select **Delete Table**.

You will not be asked to confirm the deletion.

However, if you change your mind, you can click or tap the Undo tool (located on the Quick Access toolbar) to undo the deletion.

INSERTING PICTURES

USAGE:

In addition to finding picture online, you can also insert your own personal photos from your computer.

To insert a graphic file, follow the steps outlined below:

❶ Click or tap this tool (located within the **Illustrations** section on the Insert Ribbon).

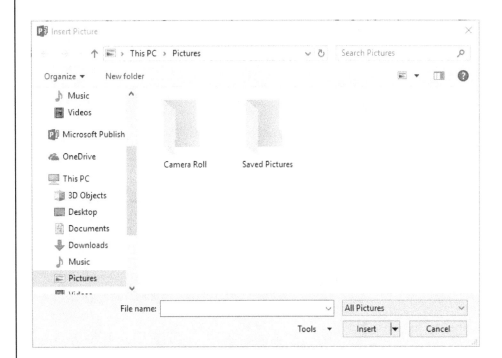

❷ From the resulting box (shown above), find the folder where your picture is stored and then select the picture itself and then click on the Insert button.

The picture should be displayed on your screen.

You may now edit it as you would any other graphic object within your publication.

Once a picture has been added to your publication, you can use the Picture Tools Format Ribbon to modify the image:

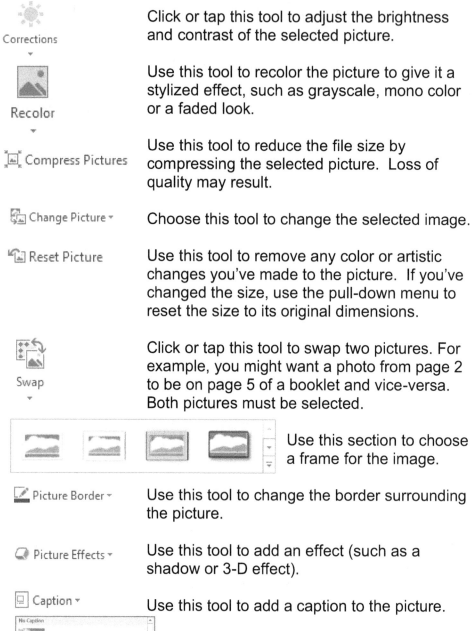

Corrections — Click or tap this tool to adjust the brightness and contrast of the selected picture.

Recolor — Use this tool to recolor the picture to give it a stylized effect, such as grayscale, mono color or a faded look.

Compress Pictures — Use this tool to reduce the file size by compressing the selected picture. Loss of quality may result.

Change Picture — Choose this tool to change the selected image.

Reset Picture — Use this tool to remove any color or artistic changes you've made to the picture. If you've changed the size, use the pull-down menu to reset the size to its original dimensions.

Swap — Click or tap this tool to swap two pictures. For example, you might want a photo from page 2 to be on page 5 of a booklet and vice-versa. Both pictures must be selected.

Use this section to choose a frame for the image.

Picture Border — Use this tool to change the border surrounding the picture.

Picture Effects — Use this tool to add an effect (such as a shadow or 3-D effect).

Caption — Use this tool to add a caption to the picture.

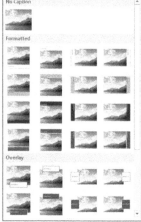

WORKING WITH BUILDING BLOCKS

USAGE:

Publisher comes with a host of its own building blocks (such as borders and accents, calendars, and advertisements) that can be added to your publication.

These professional looking objects (located within the **Building Blocks** section on the Insert Ribbon) can be inserted onto your page and then modified to look as though you created it from scratch. For example, if you have a custom table format that you've created and would like to re-use for future publications, you can save it as a building block.

To access the building blocks, switch to the Insert ribbon:

Click or tap on the category of building block you'd like to insert and then select the specific object within that category.

You can click or tap the ⌐₃ button (located along the bottom right side of the list) to display the complete list of categories.

Once inserted, the building block can be modified just as you would any other graphic object within your publication.

ADDING A BUILDING BLOCK

If you've already created an object that you would like stored as a building block to use in future publications, you can have Publisher add it to your list.

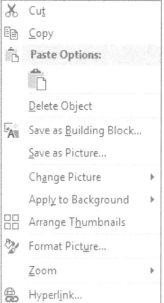

To store an object as a building block, select it and then click your **[RIGHT]** mouse button once (or tap and hold if working with a touch screen device).

From the pop-up menu, choose **Save as Building Block…**

You'll be taken to a dialog box where you can enter a name for the new building block, a description and select which gallery and category the object should be added to.

Make your selections and then click or tap OK.

PRACTICE EXERCISE

Instructions:

❶ Create a new publication.

❷ Add one of the online pictures available within Publisher.

❸ Insert a WordArt object that includes your company name.

❹ Rotate the WordArt object so that it slants slightly to the right.

❺ Insert one of the frames available within the Publisher Building Block Gallery and then customize it to add your own company name.

❻ Save and print (or preview) the publication.

❼ When done, close the file.

If You Have Time

- **Hyperlinks**
- **Working with the Master Page**
- **Preparing for Commercial Printing**

WORKING WITH HYPERLINKS

USAGE:

You can make your publication more interactive by adding hyperlinks to text or graphic objects. A hyperlink is a simple link or connection to another part of the current publication, a different file, or a Web page. More than likely, you will only add hyperlinks to publications you plan on saving as Web pages or pdfs since printed documents don't have much use for hyperlinks.

INSERTING A HYPERLINK

To insert a hyperlink, follow the steps outlined below:

❶   Select the text or object to which the hyperlink will be added.

❷   Click or tap this tool (located within the **Links** section on the Insert Ribbon).

Link

The following dialog box will be displayed:

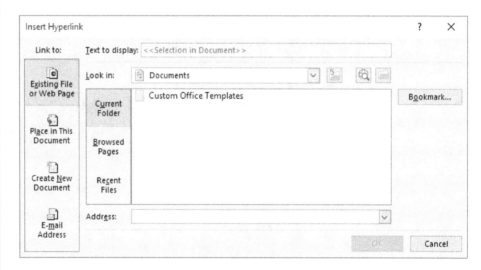

The dialog box contains the following options:

Text to display   Use this box to add or edit the text you would like displayed for the hyperlink (i.e., 'Click Here'). If you have selected text, an image or other object, this box will not be available.

Link to

Use this section (located along the left side of the dialog box) to select the type of hyperlink you wish to create.

Existing File or Web Page

Click or tap this option (the default) to create the new hyperlink from an existing file or Web page.

Place in This Document

Use this option to link the hyperlink to a location within the current document.

Create New Document

Click or tap on this option to create a new page (that doesn't exist yet) for this hyperlink. When you choose this option, you will be asked to enter a name for the new document and if you want to edit it now or later.

E-mail Address

Select this option to add a hyperlink that creates a new e-mail message when the user clicks on it. When you choose this option, you will be asked to enter the e-mail address to which the message should be sent and a default subject.

Depending on which type of link you select, the options within the remainder of this dialog box will change. For example, if you chose to link to a "Place in this document," you will need to then select which page within the document that the item should link to.

❸   Select the type of link you want to create and then fill out the options required for that link.

❹   When done, click or tap | OK |.

EDITING/REMOVING A HYPERLINK

Link

To edit an existing hyperlink or remove an unwanted one, simply select the object attached to the hyperlink and then click or tap this tool again. You'll be returned to the original dialog box where you may edit or remove the hyperlink.

WORKING WITH THE MASTER PAGE

USAGE:

When creating a publication, you may find that you would like to add a block of text (such as your company name) or graphic object (such as a company logo) that will be seen on each and every page. By adding an object to the master page, you are ensuring that the object is displayed in the same location on every page within the publication as well as any new pages you might add.

You must be careful, however, when adding background objects to existing publications because these objects can interfere with text and/or other objects already on a page. For this reason, it is better to create the master page **before** you begin adding pages.

VIEWING THE MASTER PAGE

Master Page

Click or tap this tool (located within the **Views** section on the View Ribbon) to switch to Master Page.

A blank page will be displayed along with the boundaries and layout guides. Notice that a new Ribbon has been added to your screen (labeled **Master Page**).

You may now begin adding the text items and graphic objects you would like placed on every page of your publication.

RETURNING TO NORMAL VIEW

Close Master Page

When you are done, click or tap this tool to return to normal view.

Once you have closed the master page view, you will need to access it again if you want to make any additional changes to the items you have placed on the master page.

PREPARING FOR COMMERCIAL PRINTING

USAGE:

Once your publication has been designed, you may need to send it out to a commercial printer to have it reproduced. You will need to make sure that any special fonts and/or graphics within your publication are available to the printer.

They may also require that you use a special color printing process which you can define within Publisher.

To prepare your publication for commercial printing, open the **File Ribbon**.

Select **Export**.

From the resulting window, select

 Save for a Commercial Printer

A new window is displayed (shown below).

Click or tap the first option (labeled **Commercial Press**) to select the quality of the printout.

Click or tap on the second option to choose what should be included in the package (a PDF and/or the Publisher file).

 When done, click or tap this button.

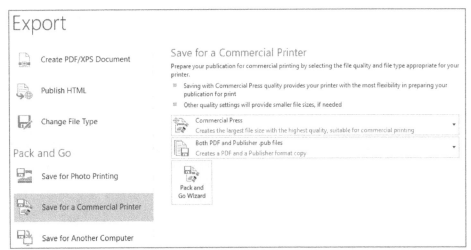

The following dialog box will be displayed:

Choose the location where the package should be stored and click or tap on the Next > button.

Publisher will create the package. Once the process is complete, the following box will be displayed:

Remove the checkmark if you don't want to print a proof of the publication. When done, click or tap OK .

www.ingramcontent.com/pod-product-compliance
Lightning Source LLC
LaVergne TN
LVHW081658050326
832903LV00026B/1819